FLAWED PROCESS

and

SECTARIAN SUBSTANCE

FLAWED PROCESS
and
SECTARIAN SUBSTANCE

Analytic and Critical Perspectives
on the United Church of Christ
General Synod Pronouncement
"Christian Faith: Economic
Life and Justice"

W. Widick Schroeder

EXPLORATION PRESS
Chicago, Illinois

Studies in Ministry and Parish Life

Printed in the United States of America.

Exploration Press
Chicago Theological Seminary
5757 S. University Ave.
Chicago, Illinois 60637

ISBN: Cloth: 0-913552-41-0
Paper: 0-913552-42-9
Library of Congress Catalog Card Number: 89-81461

CONTENTS

TABLES

CHARTS

PREFACE

This study examines the evolution of a United Church of Christ General Synod pronouncement on economic matters from the initial phases of its formulation in 1980 to its adoption by the Seventeenth General Synod of the United Church of Christ in 1989.

I became tangentially involved in the process itself when I served as a member of a United Church of Christ Pension Boards committee in 1988. Its initial assignment was to draft a response to the study paper "Christian Faith and Economic Life" developed by a committee called the Theology and Economics Covenant Group. For reasons detailed in the body of this volume, the Pension Boards' committee did not respond to the study paper. Instead, it developed its own statement on the Christian movement and economic life.

I also presented a three-minute statement to the Seventeenth General Synod committee assigned to consider the three proposed pronouncements on economic matters. In that statement, I urged the committee to reject all three proposed pronouncements because they embodied a too narrowly conceived orthopraxis. This suggestion was obviously not persuasive, for the committee reported favorably and the General Synod adopted the pronouncement examined in detail in the body of this volume.

When evaluating this study, the reader should take these involvements into account. I have been an observer-participant in the pronouncement process, but my participant role was minimal. I do not think my marginal involvement in the process has seriously impacted my ability to analyze the process or the substance of the documents, but others may differ with my judgment on this matter.

As one who has had a long interest in the sociology of religious organizations and who has a strong constructive bias in favor of congregational polity for religious bodies, I became very interested in the process by which General Synod sponsored documents are developed. Consequently, after my minor involvement in the process, I decided to conduct a study of this pronouncement's evolution.

The study analyzes both the process of pronouncement development and the substance of the various documents. The content of the documents produced by the various committees is examined comparatively to discern divergences and convergences between the several documents. The composition of the committees drafting the several documents is correlated with the substance of their work.

I hold that fact and value are interrelated because fully concrete events are constituted by their evaluation of other things. Consequently, both analytic and constructive work are legitimate in sociological and socio-cultural analyses.

I critically assess both the process by which the pronouncement was adopted and also the substance of the adopted pronouncement. I have dealt primarily with the substance of the adopted pronouncement because it represents the expressed view of the United Church of Christ General Synod.

As the reader will discover, I am quite critical both of the process by which this pronouncement was developed and also the substance of the pronouncement. In my judgment, the committees drafting the various pronouncements were too narrowly based. As a result the pronouncement advanced a sectarian interpretation of the Christian movement and of American economic life.

This investigation is an interesting case study in the exploration of a facet of a broad movement of a denomination from a more centrist position in American life to a more marginal one. If the actions on this pronouncement are representative of the broader views of people employed by national agencies and instrumentalities who sponsored this pronouncement, members of their respective boards who approved it, and the delegates to the General Synod who adopted it, salient leadership groups are insensitive to congregational polity, entertain narrowly conceived theological viewpoints, and are situated in the left wing of American political life. On these counts, their views contrast with the beliefs and expectations of very significant segments of the membership of the United Church of Christ. So long as their actions are ignored, the consequences of these divergences may be minimal. If local congregations were to pay serious attention to the views represented in this pronouncement, substantial disagreement would likely surface.

This pattern of increasing cognitive and affective dissonance between significant leadership groups and laity is manifest in varying degree in several denominations in the United States. (Included are bodies such as the American Baptists, Presbyterians,

Episcopalians, Lutherans, and United Methodists.) Many of the emerging leaders in these denominations were shaped by the Civil Rights Movement and the Vietnam War protests in the 1960s. Appropriating various forms of liberation theology, which has strong egalitarian emphases, focuses on orthopraxis (right conduct) and sharply blurs or obliterates distinctions between the community of faith and the community of politics, these religious professionals occupy significant leadership roles in theological seminaries and some parts of denominational bureaucracies. Because of the tempering effect of leadership roles in local congregations, they are not as visible in most local church settings. The exceptions are those few highly intentional fellowships whose penchant for certain forms of social action has produced relatively homogenous membership sharing the basic intentionality of the local congregation.

As a result of this highly visible national leadership in the former "main-line" denominations, the Roman Catholic Church and evangelical Protestant groups have become relatively more centrist in the American experience. In its pastoral letters on war and peace and on the American economy, the National Conference of Catholic Bishops has advanced more balanced and centrist views on economic and political issues than have most of the former "main-line" Protestant churches.

On the short run, these movements at the national level will not have much impact on church membership, but long-term patterns are more problematic. Unless the United Church of Christ national bodies sponsoring this pronouncement display more sensitivity to congregational polity and to the legitimacy of contrasting prudential judgments on political economy and public policy issues, some realignment of church membership may develop. Those desiring a "purer" and/or "more highly committed" membership may desire such a development. Those seeing religious institutions as sustainers as well as critics of higher civilization and the public realm will lament such a development.

I want to express my appreciation to John Ordway and Wayne Owens of the United Church of Christ Pension Boards for stimulating my interest in this project, to Stephen J. Davidson and Kenneth B. Smith of the Chicago Theological Seminary for inviting me to make public presentations of earlier drafts of this study, and to Max Havlick for his most valuable editorial and secretarial assistance.

W. Widick Schroeder
Chicago Theological Seminary

INTRODUCTION

In July 1989 the Seventeenth General Synod of the United Church of Christ adopted a pronouncement on economic issues. Entitled "Christian Faith: Economic Life and Justice," the General Synod's adoption of this pronouncement culminated a process begun in December 1980. At that time a small group of United Church of Christ theologians and economists formed a Theology and Economics Covenant Group. According to their own testimony, the group covenanted together, "struggling to be obedient to Jesus Christ, to join the search for new economic theories and policies more faithful to the gospel."[1]

As it happened, most members of this initial group were very critical of American democratic capitalism and promoted public policies which, if adopted, would move toward a democratic socialist form of political economy. They set the tone for a series of documents on the Christian movement and economic issues that emerged from various United Church of Christ committees in the next eight and one-half years, culminating in a General Synod pronouncement on the Christian faith and economic issues in July 1989.

In the United Church of Christ, "A pronouncement is a statement of Christian conviction on a matter of moral or social principle and has been adopted by a two-thirds vote of a General Synod. It is based on biblical, theological and ethical grounds."[2] Because the General Synod speaks *to* the churches, not *for* the churches, a pronouncement is not binding on a local congregation. Indeed, a local congregation may ignore, modify, accept, or reject any or all pronouncements adopted by a General Synod. Pronouncements do, however, legitimate and sometimes shape the work of members of national agencies and conferences.

The first chapter of this study considers the context in which the discussions have evolved by addressing briefly the question of congregational polity and its impact on the substance and shape of the discussions. The second chapter outlines the process leading to the formulation of five publicly distributed committee-developed documents furthering the discussion of the Christian faith and economic issues. The third chapter examines the substance of these documents. The fourth chapter considers the General Synod's revision and adoption of the pronouncement entitled "Christian Faith: Economic Life and Justice." The concluding chapter offers some critical reflections on the process by which the proposed pronouncement was developed and acted upon by the Seventeenth General Synod of the United Church of Christ in July 1989. It also makes a critical assessment of the substance of the pronouncement.

The *first* public document, which was prepared by the Economics and Theology Covenant Group and distributed in January 1987 by the Hunger Action Office of the United Church Board for World Ministries, is a "study paper" titled *Christian Faith and Economic Life.* The paper was developed to contribute "to a pronouncement for the Seventeenth General Synod of the United Church of Christ."[3] The *second* document is a statement titled *The Market System and American Democratic Polity: Reflections in the Light of Covenantal Tradition*, developed and distributed in February 1989 by The Pension Boards Trustees, United Church of Christ. The *third* document, which was distributed at the end of March 1989, is a proposed pronouncement titled "Christian Faith and Economic Life," recommended by the Office for Church in Society, with the concurrence of the United Church Board for Homeland Ministries, and the United Church Board for World Ministries. The *fourth* document, also distributed at the end of March 1989, is a proposed pronouncement titled "Christian Faith and Economic Justice," recommended by the Commission for Racial Justice and the Council for Racial and Ethnic Ministries of the United Church of Christ. The *fifth* document, sent to General Synod delegates just before the Synod convened in late June 1989, is a proposed pronouncement titled "Christian Faith: Economic Life and Justice." It was sponsored by the United Church Board for World Ministries, the United Church Board for Homeland Ministries, the Office for Church in Society, and the Commission for Racial Justice. The cover note asked the Synod to use this text for its deliberations rather than the two previously circulated proposed pronouncements just cited. It was developed by a committee dominated by staff members of the groups who developed the other two proposed pronouncements. This text was, in fact, the one which served as the basis of the deliberations of the General Synod committee assigned to deal with the proposed pronouncements on the Christian faith and economic life.

Three of these texts are reproduced in the appendix of this volume. The documents are: the Pension Boards Trustees' statement, *The Market System and American Democratic Polity: Reflections in the Light of Covenantal Tradition*; the proposed pronouncement, "Christian Faith and Economic Justice," recommended by the Commission for Racial Justice and the Council for Racial and Ethnic Ministries of the United Church of Christ; and the adopted pronouncement, "Christian Faith: Economic Life and Justice."[4]

These texts were selected because they represent contrasting views on the topic. The first two texts reflect very sharp differences in their interpretations of a market economy. The third text is largely an outgrowth of the study paper and the proposed pronouncement "Christian Faith and Economic Life," modified by some material drawn from the proposed pronouncement "Christian Faith and Economic Justice." It is more temperate in its critique of a market economy than the "Christian Faith and Economic Justice" proposed pronouncement, but it is much more critical of American democratic capitalism than the Pension Board Trustees' statement. Because this text is the one adopted by the General Synod, it is the most important of the three documents. It is critiqued at length in the last chapter of this volume.

CHAPTER I

Congregational Polity and Denominational Initiatives

The United Church of Christ is a denomination with a congregational form of polity. This polity has affected the process leading to three proposed pronouncements on the Christian faith and economic issues submitted for the consideration of the 1989 General Synod of the United Church of Christ. According to the Constitution of the United Church of Christ, local churches, associations, conferences, national agencies and instrumentalities, and the General Synod are autonomous within their own spheres. Even though the Constitution is unequivocally clear on the principle of local congregational autonomy, some people in the denomination desire a greater sense of covenantal connectedness than do others. Some celebrate the theological diversity, tolerance, and plurality which congregational polity permits more enthusiastically than do others. Critics are concerned about the fracturing of the unity of the church, the diminution of covenantal relations, the laxness and variety of doctrinal interpretation and the excessive individualism they experience in the UCC.

Because of the multiple centers of initiative in the UCC, loosely coordinated but dominated by no one group, special interest groups abound, seeking to promote their causes. Although it has no direct constitutional authority over local congregations, the General Synod, a biennial national assembly of between 675 and 725 delegates selected by the 39 Conferences of the United Church of Christ, often becomes a focal point for persons and groups promoting particular viewpoints, causes, and/or programs.[1]

The number of General Synod delegates from each conference is based on the number of persons who have membership in the local churches of the conference. The composition of the delegations is shaped by a quota system which has evolved over a period of time. Except in conferences having only three delegates, at least 50 percent of the delegates must be lay people. In addition the delegations should be representative of racial and ethnic persons (African-Americans, Hispanics, American Indians, Asian-Americans, and Pacific Islanders), women and youth. In this last instance, at least 20 percent of the delegates of each conference must be under 30 years of age at the time their terms begin.

As noted in the Introduction, the General Synod speaks *to* the churches, not *for* the churches. Under the constitution, a local congregation may affirm, qualify, reject, or ignore any of the General Synod's pronouncements. Synod action provides notoriety and frequently funding for particular programs and/or interest groups addressed in adopted pronouncements. It also legitimates actions by the agencies cited in the given pronouncement.

As will be detailed in the following chapter, the denomination's congregational form of polity has facilitated the development of five committee-developed documents on the Christian faith and economic issues by five different bodies with some overlapping membership.

To help the reader trace the development of the various documents, the sponsoring body or bodies and the date of distribution of the five committee-developed formulations are summarized in Chart 1 at the end of this chapter.

While these multiple initiatives are not unique to denominations with a congregational form of polity, this form of polity does inherently produce multiple centers of authority. Because of the autonomy granted each entity within its own sphere, no entity can formulate a definitive denominational viewpoint. For this reason, on a given topic or issue, local congregations, conferences, and various national agencies may entertain substantial differences in interpretation.

CHART 1. THE DEVELOPMENT OF DOCUMENTS LEADING TO THE ADOPTED PRONOUNCEMENT, "CHRISTIAN FAITH: ECONOMIC LIFE AND JUSTICE"

Title of Document	Date of Distribution	Drafting Group	Sponsoring Agencies
Christian Faith and Economic Life Study Paper	Jan. 1987	Economics and Theology Covenant Group (sponsored by the Office for Church in Society, United Church Board for World Ministries, and the United Church Board for Homeland Ministries)	Hunger Action Office, United Church Board for World Ministries (responsible for distributing study paper)
The Market System and American Democratic Polity: Reflections in the Light of Covenantal Tradition Statement	Feb. 1989	United Church of Christ Pension Boards' Committee on Reflections in the Light of Covenantal Tradition	Pension Boards Trustees, United Church of Christ
Proposed Pronouncement, "Christian Faith and Economic Life"	Apr. 1989	Pronouncement Committee	Office for Church in Society with the concurrence of the United Church Board for Homeland Ministries and the United Church Board for World Ministries
Proposed Pronouncement "Christian Faith and Economic Justice"	Apr. 1989	Representatives of Commission for Racial Justice and the Council for Racial and Ethnic Ministries	Commission for Racial Justice and the Council for Racial and Ethnic Ministries, United Church of Christ
Proposed Pronouncement, "Christian Faith: Economic Life and Justice"	June 1989	Chair of Pronouncement Committee, non-staff representative of Council for Racial and Ethnic Ministries, staff members of the United Church Board for Homeland Ministries, United Church Board for World Ministries, the Office for Church in Society, and the Commission for Racial Justice	Board of Directors or Executive Committees of the United Church Board for Homeland Ministries, the United Church Board for World Ministries, the Office for Church in Society, and the Commission for Racial Justice
Adopted Pronouncement, "Christian Faith: Economic Life and Justice"	July 1989	Committee of Delegates to the Seventeenth General Synod, United Church of Christ	Seventeenth General Synod, United Church of Christ

CHAPTER II

Committee Composition and Statement Development

1. THE STUDY PAPER, *CHRISTIAN FAITH AND ECONOMIC LIFE*

The evolution of the proposed Synod pronouncements on the Christian faith and economic matters illustrates the process of special interest group initiatives encouraged by the UCC's congregational polity, for a relatively small number of highly committed persons dominated the process leading to the pronouncement on economic issues at the 1989 General Synod.

The evolution of the pronouncement on economic matters adopted at the General Synod in the summer of 1989 took almost a decade. In December 1980, a self-selected group of United Church of Christ theologians and economists organized an Economics and Theology Covenant Group. This group "covenanted together, 'struggling to be obedient to Jesus Christ, to join the search for new economic theories and policies more faithful to the gospel'."[1]

This group's work led to a resolution at the 1983 General Synod jointly sponsored by two national denominational agencies, the Office for Church in Society and the United Church Board for World Ministries, to develop a proposed pronouncement on economic matters. The resolution adopted by the 1983 synod reads as follows:

> BE IT RESOLVED that the Fourteenth General Synod of the United Church of Christ requests the Office for Church in Society and the United Church Board for World Ministries, through their joint Economics and Theology Covenant Group, to convene a broadly representative group of economists, theologians, church leaders, leaders of organizations of poor and working people and others to study these matters (issues of economics and theology), and to present to the Fifteenth General Synod a Proposed Pronouncement, including:
>
> 1. An analysis of the global economic crisis and the impact and function of economic relationships on the whole of life;
>
> 2. The findings resulting from their study of economic theory, history, Christian Scripture and theology; and
>
> 3. An articulation of a public theology of economics.
>
> BE IT FURTHER RESOLVED that this Proposed Pronouncement be accompanied by a Proposal for Action which shall include:
>
> 1. A proposal for strengthening the teaching ministry of the church on economics and theology; and
>
> 2. An appropriate response by the United Church of Christ.[2]

The evolution of the self-initiated voluntary Economics and Theology Covenant Group, established in 1980, to a committee sponsored jointly by the United Church Board for World Ministries and the Office for Church in Society in 1983 illustrates the way in which special interest groups legitimate themselves in the United Church of Christ.

This process of legitimation continued after the adoption of the 1983 General Synod resolution. Staff persons in the United

Church Board for World Ministries and the Office for Church in Society consulted with the co-chairpersons of the Economics and Theology Covenant Group to expand "the membership of the Economics and Theology Covenant Group to include representatives of groups identified in the General Synod resolution and the perspective of overseas partners of the United Church of Christ."[3] During this time period, the United Church Board for Homeland Ministries became another co-sponsoring national denominational agency for the Economics and Theology Covenant Group.

As the General Synod mandate "to convene a broadly representative group of economists, theologians, church leaders, leaders of organizations of poor and working people and others to study these matters (issues of economic and theology)" was quite vague, staff people had substantial latitude in the selection of the reconstituted membership of the Economics and Theology Covenant Group to prepare a study paper contributing to a proposed pronouncement. An analysis of the composition of the group helps one understand the study paper's sharply critical attitude toward the workings of a market economy and its proposed much greater state and international agency involvement in economic affairs. Had the group been differently balanced, it probably would have advanced different prudential judgments about the best means to alleviate poverty and material deprivation and desirable forms of political economy.

The reconstituted and formally legitimated Economics and Theology Covenant Group had 25 members. In addition, four staff people from denominational agencies gave part-time support to the group. Based on the titles cited for committee members, 72 percent of the group (excluding the four ordained staff people) were ordained people, and 28 percent were lay people. Twenty-eight percent were female, and 72 percent were male. The occupational distribution of the group is summarized in Table 1.

A steering committee of the Covenant Group met more frequently than the entire body, and it probably set the agenda for the discussions and deliberations for the larger group. Its composition is shown in Table 2.

Given the study paper's ambivalently negative assessment of large corporations and of a market economy set in the context of a nation with a democratic polity, the paucity of UCC lay people affiliated with for-profit companies and corporations in the group

TABLE 1. OCCUPATIONAL DISTRIBUTION OF THE MEMBERS OF THE ECONOMICS AND THEOLOGY COVENANT GROUP

Institute or Specialized Ministries (n = 9)		36%
Professors (n = 9)		36%
Seminary (n = 5)	20%	
Economics (n = 3)	12%	
Philosophy (n = 1)	4%	
Ministers of Parish Churches (n = 4)		16%
Lawyers (n = 2)		8%
Management Trainee (n = 1)		4%

Source: *Christian Faith and Economic Life*, p. iv.

TABLE 2. OCCUPATIONAL DISTRIBUTION OF THE STEERING COMMITTEE OF THE ECONOMICS AND THEOLOGY COVENANT GROUP

UCC National Staff (n = 4)		31%
Professors (n = 6)		46%
Seminary (n = 4)	31%	
Economics (n = 2)	15%	
Specialized Ministries (n = 3)		23%

Source: *Christian Faith and Economic Life*, p. iv.

is especially striking. Similarly striking is the paucity of UCC lay people who are mainline economists, political scientists, employees of city, county, state, or federal governments, and elected public officials. Had such people been included in the expanded Economics and Theology Covenant Group, the interpretations in the study paper might well have been more sympathetic to a market economy set in the context of a society with a democratic form of government than was, in fact, the case.

This study paper was circulated to the churches in January 1987.

2. THE PROPOSED PRONOUNCEMENT, "CHRISTIAN FAITH AND ECONOMIC LIFE"

After the study paper *Christian Faith and Economic Life* was completed, the same three sponsoring bodies, i.e., the United Church Board for World Ministries, the Office for Church in Society, and the United Church Board for Homeland Ministries, established an Economics and Theology Pronouncement Committee to develop a proposed pronouncement for the 1989 General Synod. (The development process had taken so long that the proposed pronouncement was not ready for the 1985 or 1987 General Synods.) The occupational distribution of the members of the Pronouncement Committee is shown in Table 3.

TABLE 3. OCCUPATIONAL DISTRIBUTION OF THE MEMBERS OF THE ECONOMICS AND THEOLOGY PRONOUNCEMENT COMMITTEE

Specialized Ministries (all program people for national or conference instrumentalities) (n = 6)		41%
Professors (n = 6)		35%
Seminary (n = 4)	24%	
Economics (n = 2)	11%	
Local Pastors (n = 1)		6%
Conference Ministers (n = 1)		6%
Retail Business Executives (n = 1)		6%
Bank Executive (retired) (n = 1)		6%

Source: Membership List provided by the Economics and Theology Pronouncement Committee.

Of the 17 committee members, eight had been members of the Economics and Theology Covenant Group which had prepared the study paper *Christian Faith and Economic Life* leading to the proposed pronouncement "Christian Faith and Economic Life." All three staff members and the chair of the committee had been members of the earlier group. Given the dynamics of committee processes, because of this large company of overlapping participants the same people who wrote the original study paper also greatly influenced the tenor of the process and substance of the proposed pronouncement.

This proposed pronouncement, along with the proposed pronouncement "The Christian Faith and Economic Justice," was mailed to General Synod delegates and to the churches in late March/early April 1989. It was subsequently withdrawn in favor of the final document to be considered, "Christian Faith: Economic Life and Justice."

3. THE PENSION BOARDS' STATEMENT, *THE MARKET SYSTEM AND AMERICAN DEMOCRATIC POLITY: REFLECTIONS IN THE LIGHT OF COVENANTAL TRADITION*

Meantime, the Board of Trustees of the Pension Boards of the United Church of Christ decided to make a response to the *Christian Faith and Economic Life* study paper prepared by the Economics and Theology Covenant Group. Given the workings of quasi-voluntary bodies, a year had elapsed between the time of the publication of the study paper in January 1987 and the constitution of the Pension Boards' Response Committee in January 1988. By the time this committee was functioning, the study paper was passé, for the Pronouncement Committee was already drafting a proposed pronouncement. Consequently, instead of responding directly to the study paper, the committee decided to draft a statement of its own to contribute to the discussions on the Christian faith and economic issues leading to the 1989 General Synod deliberations. This document is much more sympathetic toward a market economy functioning in a society with a democratic polity than is the study paper or any of the three proposed pronouncements submitted to the General Synod. Its prudential judgments about the means to alleviate poverty and material deprivation differ substantially from those in the study paper or in any of the proposed pronouncements. The statement was mailed to United Church of Christ clergy in February 1989.

As was the case with the Economics and Theology Covenant Group, the composition of the Pension Boards' committee will help one understand the tenor and substance of this document. The occupational distribution of the members of the committee is shown in Table 4.

TABLE 4. OCCUPATIONAL DISTRIBUTION OF THE UCC PENSION BOARDS' COMMITTEE ON REFLECTIONS IN THE LIGHT OF COVENANTAL TRADITION

Specialized Ministries (all Pension Boards staff) (n = 4)	27%
Conference Ministers (n = 1)	7%
Economist and V.P. Major Brokerage Firm (n = 1)	7%
Seminary Professor (n = 1)	7%
Local Pastors (n = 2)	13%
Business Executives, CEO's (n = 2)	13%
Bank Executives (n = 2)	13%
College or Seminary Presidents (n = 2)	13%

Source: *The Market System and American Democratic Polity: Reflections in the Light of Covenantal Tradition*, p. 15.

In contrast to the Economics and Theology Covenant Group, about half the members of the Pension Boards' committee were people who held or had held senior positions in corporate, academic, and governmental institutions. Academics were less represented, and no spokespersons for organizations of the poor and working groups were on the committee. Thus this committee was unbalanced in a different direction than was the Economics and Theology Covenant Group.

4. THE PROPOSED PRONOUNCEMENT, "CHRISTIAN FAITH AND ECONOMIC JUSTICE"

Although the General Synod delegates in 1983 had envisaged a single proposed pronouncement on economic matters (originally scheduled for submission to the General Synod in 1985), their requested proposed pronouncement was not the only one on economic issues to be submitted to the 1989 General Synod. Persuaded that the proposed pronouncement on the "Christian Faith and Economic Life" was written from the perspective of the white middle and upper class majority on the committee and did not adequately address racism in economic life, the Commission for Racial Justice and the Council for Racial and Ethnic Ministries submitted their own proposed pronouncement on economic matters.[4] Believing the Pronouncement Committee's proposed pronouncement did not deal adequately with economic justice, the representatives of these bodies who were on the Pronouncement Committee encouraged these bodies to develop another proposed pronouncement. No public hearings were held, but, according to the deputy director of the Commission for Racial Justice, ". . . all of the member caucuses within COREM [an acronym for Council for Racial and Ethnic Ministries] did have extensive input into the document."[5] This proposed pronouncement, titled "Christian Faith and Economic Justice," was mailed to General Synod delegates and to the churches in the late March/early April 1989 mailing with the "Christian Faith and Economic Life" proposed pronouncement.

Both the Commission for Racial Justice and the Council for Racial and Ethnic Ministries were created by the General Synod. The Commission for Racial Justice is composed of 15 persons appointed by the President of the Church from a list of candidates developed through a complex process. The majority of its members must be African-American. It is responsible to the General Synod, which determines its funding.

The Council for Racial and Ethnic Ministries is composed of ten persons drawn from five groups. Each group selects two representatives who are accountable to the groups who send them. The groups include: Pacific Island and Asian American Ministry, the Council for Hispanic Ministries, the Council for American Indian Ministries, United Black Christians, and Ministers for Racial and Social Justice. It is funded by the General Synod, contingent upon its accountability to the Executive Council of the General Synod.

Whites constituted a small minority of the people drafting this proposed pronouncement. Persons committed to various forms of "social action" ministries dominated the group. Given the complex nominating procedures, those whites in the sponsoring groups were undoubtedly very sympathetic to the viewpoints being developed. Thus the group drafting this proposed pronouncement was unbalanced in yet another direction.

5. THE PROPOSED PRONOUNCEMENT, "CHRISTIAN FAITH: ECONOMIC LIFE AND JUSTICE"

Conflict and disagreement between members of the Pronouncement Committee had led to the submission of two proposed pronouncements on the Christian faith and economic matters. Subsequent to the mailing of the two proposed pronouncements to General Synod delegates and to the churches, a committee largely composed of staff representatives of the five bodies sponsoring the two proposed pronouncements met to reconcile their differences. Undoubtedly many who were committed to the passage of a proposed pronouncement on the Christian faith and economic matters were uneasy about delegates voting on two proposed pronouncements on the same topic. Both were controversial, so split voting might jeopardize passage of either. Passage of both would seem incongruous.

This committee developed a third proposed pronouncement, "Christian Faith: Economic Life and Justice" which in the minds of these committee members represented "a synthesis of the perspectives of the two pronouncements, and by doing so, provides a more adequate and comprehensive understanding of the relationship of faith to economics." (From the text of a "Resolution on the Christian Faith: Economic Life and Justice [*sic*] Pronouncement." This head was in error, for the resolution referred to a "Proposed Pronouncement" at the time it was submitted.)

No hearings were held on this proposed pronouncement nor were the members of the original Pronouncement Committee fully consulted about this new proposed pronouncement. Because of the very late distribution of this proposed pronouncement, local churches or conferences were not invited to respond to it.

The Board of Directors or Executive Committees of the United Church Board for World Ministries, the United Church Board for Homeland Ministries, the Office for Church in Society, and the Commission for Racial Justice endorsed this proposed pronouncement. The endorsing bodies asked the General Synod to substitute this proposed pronouncement for the other two proposed pronouncements sent earlier to delegates and to the churches.

The occupational distribution of the committee drafting this proposed pronouncement is shown in Table 5. As the table shows, denominational staff people dominated this drafting committee.

TABLE 5. OCCUPATIONAL DISTRIBUTION OF THE COMMITTEE DRAFTING THE PROPOSED PRONOUNCEMENT, "CHRISTIAN FAITH: ECONOMIC LIFE AND JUSTICE"

Specialized Ministries (n = 7)		78%
UCC Board for World Ministries (n = 1)	11%	
UCC Board for Homeland Ministries (n = 1)	11%	
Office for Church and Society (n = 3)	33%	
Commission for Racial Justice (n = 2)	11%	
University Professor (Chair of Pronouncement Committee, "Christian Faith and Economic Life") (n = 1)		11%
Representative of Council for Racial and Ethnic Ministries (n = 1)		11%

Source: List supplied by the Committee.

A third of the members represented the Commission for Racial Justice and the Council for Ethnic and Racial Ministries, the sponsoring agencies for the "Christian Faith and Economic Justice" proposed pronouncement. Another third came from the Office for Church in Society. The two largest agencies, the United Church Board for World Ministries and the United

Church Board for Homeland Ministries, each had one delegate.[6] The chairperson and three United Church of Christ staff people had been on the Theology and Economics Covenant Group which developed the study paper and on the original Pronouncement Committee which had drafted the proposed pronouncement, "Christian Faith and Economic Life." An additional person had been on the Pronouncement Committee. The other four persons had not been involved in other phases of the deliberations. The more centrist people who were underrepresented in early phases of the pronouncement process were totally absent from this final drafting and legitimating body.

INTEREST GROUP INTERACTION

This detailing of the process of proposed pronouncement formulations illumines the complex interplay of people and interest groups shaping the development of the proposed pronouncements. In the self-selected way depicted in the analysis of the proposed pronouncement process, special interest groups interacted with each other. Because UCC committees, boards, and special interest groups seek a consensus on their formulations and/or proposed projects (an ideal not, of course, always realized), they must limit their breadth of representation. In addition, they often seek specialized expertise consonant with the dominant viewpoint of the committee or board.

In the main, clergy employed by denominational bodies and theological institutions dominated the development process. Local pastors and lay people have been underrepresented. Staff people associated with national bodies occupied a salient position in the process, particularly in its final phases.

Education was less highly prized than promotion, for each group advanced its own views on very complex issues. Over all consensus formation was muted, and the interplay of interest groups was highlighted. (In fact, as the analysis of the substance of the documents in the following chapter will show, there is no way to attain a consensus on the contrasting views developed by these various bodies, for some of the views developed by the various groups are mutually exclusive.)

Interest group interaction was especially evident in the late submission of the new proposed pronouncement "Christian Faith:

Economic Life and Justice." Bypassing and/or short-cutting established procedures, denominational executives in the five bodies sponsoring the final form of the proposed pronouncement submitted it to General Synod delegates on the eve of the General Synod.

Lay and local clergy input was virtually absent in the development of the final form of the proposed pronouncement. Non-whites occupied central roles in these negotiations. Denominational executives seemed preoccupied in developing a draft which would overcome the split between whites and minorities that had taken place between representatives of the various national bodies in the Pronouncement Committee.[7] One wonders what compromises might have taken place if the few persons on the Pronouncement Committee with an ambivalently positive attitude toward a market economy had sought to submit an alternative proposed pronouncement embodying the ideas included in the Pension Boards Trustees' statement. Because no such group emerged, the final proposed pronouncement represented a "compromise" between those unequivocally rejecting a market economy and those strongly critical of a market economy.

Two other factors, not directly related to these deliberations on the Christian faith and economic matters, contributed both to the complexity of those negotiations and to General Synod action. First, one of the negotiators of the final pronouncement was an African-American woman who was among the finalists in the competition for the presidency of the denomination. The nominating committee finally passed her over and recommended a white man. She was subsequently nominated from the floor at the General Synod, but the nominating committee's recommended candidate defeated her. African-American sensitivity on this matter probably affected these negotiations and the vote on the matter at the General Synod. Second, a major controversy over the proposed relocation of the national headquarters of the United Church of Christ occupied the attention of almost all denominational executives within these agencies. While probably not as significant as the first factor, it is important. Both the presidential election and the final resolution of the headquarters issue were probably more important to most of the General Synod delegates than the proposed pronouncement on economic matters. In the complex interplay of interest group with interest group at the General Synod, some aware of African-American sensitivity on the presidential issue may have decided to support the new proposed pronouncement to show concern for minorities in the denomination.

CHAPTER III

The Substance of the Documents

INTRODUCTION

In this chapter, the substance of the five public documents noted in the preceding chapter is explored. The first document is the Economics and Theology Covenant Group's study paper *Christian Faith and Economic Life.* The second is the Pension Boards Trustees' statement, *The Market System and American Democratic Polity: Reflections in the Light of Covenantal Tradition.* The third is the proposed pronouncement, "Christian Faith and Economic Life," developed by the Pronouncement Committee emerging from the Economics and Theology Covenant Group and recommended by the Office for Church in Society with the concurrence of the United Board for Homeland Ministries and the United Church Board for World Ministries. The fourth is the proposed pronouncement, "Christian Faith and Economic Justice," developed and sponsored by the Commission for Racial Justice and the Council for Racial and Ethnic Ministries of the United Church of Christ. The fifth is the proposed pronouncement "Christian Faith: Economic Life and Justice," recommended by the United Church Board for Homeland Ministries, the United Church Board for World Ministries, the Office for Church in Society, and the Commission for Racial

Justice in cooperation with the Council for Racial and Ethnic Ministries. As noted, the sponsoring bodies asked the Seventeenth General Synod to substitute this proposed pronouncement for the other two proposed pronouncements examined in this chapter. The revised form of this proposed pronouncement which the General Synod adopted is summarized in Chapter IV and is examined critically in Chapter V. Chart 2 summarizes comparatively selected issues in the five documents and in the adopted pronouncement. It is attached at the end of Chapter IV.

1. THE STUDY PAPER, *CHRISTIAN FAITH AND ECONOMIC LIFE*

The 45-page, 303-paragraph study paper is the longest of the five documents distributed to the churches. It set the tone for much of the subsequent discussions and many of its motifs appeared in the proposed pronouncement "Christian Faith and Economic Life" and in the adopted pronouncement "Christian Faith: Economic Life and Justice." Like most Protestant documents, it is neither internally consistent nor systematically coherent, but it draws substantially on interpretations developed by various strands of what has come to be called "liberation theology." Most liberation theologians are highly critical of market-oriented economies, and many propose democratic socialism as a more desired mode of political economy. Most stress the primacy of praxis and are more prone to promote proper action rather than proper belief.

The thought of Jürgen Moltmann, a non-Marxist German theologian and proponent of democratic socialism, informs the particular Protestant version of liberation theology appearing in parts of the study paper.[1] Because Douglas Meeks, one of the co-chairs of the Economics and Theology Covenant Group which prepared this paper, is a translator and sympathetic interpreter of Moltmann, this influence is not surprising.[2]

Moltmann's influence is evident in the following motifs appearing in the study paper: (1) The strong focus on biblical metaphors, with the concomitant minimization of natural law and appeal to other warrants for one's views. (2) The emphasis on the futurity of God's action in history, with the concomitant minimization of efforts to assess the likely consequences of particular proposals for the body politic based on knowledge of the way in which events in the causal past have characteristically effected economic and political life. (3) The relative optimism about the prospects for the harmony of life with life following the proposed major transformation of the political economy. (4) The view of the church as a mature Spirit-filled community.

Some liberation theologians, particularly those from Asia, Africa, and Latin America, are deeply influenced by Marxist modes of social analysis. In their social analyses, Marxist informed analysts are prone to divide humankind into polar groups based on social and/or biological characteristics. Status, class, race, sex and/or nation-states are the commonly designated polar types. One group is characterized as the oppressor and the other as the oppressed. Sharp social conflict between the groups is generally viewed as inevitable.[3]

Marxist informed analysts often advance dependent capitalism theories to explain the differential wealth of nations. They claim that countries with market economies are wealthy because they exploit other countries. In this context, they view so-called "first world" countries as the oppressors, and they view other nations as the oppressed. They are very critical of multi-national corporations, which they also view as oppressors.[4]

Marxist interpretations appear in parts of the study paper, but they are generally sharply qualified and modified. Some committee members related to the United Church Board for World Ministries and its overseas partners probably advanced the Marxist modes of social analysis, for this interpretation has been fashionable in some World Council of Churches circles. Nonetheless, in the complex dynamics of the committee process other viewpoints were more salient.

A third influence is the engagement-reflection model of theological social ethics. Also focused strongly on practice, this model of action and subsequent theological reflection has been fashionable among many specialized mission funded urban ministry workers in the U.S. during the past two or three decades. (About a third of the committee members had done urban mission work.)

Rooted originally in the work of H. Richard Niebuhr, Karl Barth, and others, the model encouraged people to act responsibly in the contexts in which they found themselves.[5] A dialectic between action and reflection was developed. An agent asked what God was demanding of him/her in a given situation. After prayerfully seeking to determine God's intent for one (often in the context of Bible study), the person then responded. After this action, the person reflected about what he/she had done and what God now required. The dialectic proceeded in this fashion from situation to situation.

This informing theory was intermeshed with the lives of those affirming it. Often, these specialized mission-funded urban ministry workers appropriated balance-of-power strategies associated with the Christian realism of Reinhold Niebuhr and theories of community organization associated with Saul Alinsky and the Industrial Areas Foundation.[6] In the main, they sought to enhance the power of the dispossessed in the effort to attain greater social justice. They rarely, if ever, undertook sophisticated macro economic analysis, for they had no expertise in economic theory. Such analyses would not likely have entered into the "reflection" portion of their engagement-reflection model of social action.

Finally, other sections of the study paper reflect different perspectives. Some mainline economic analyses and other theological perspectives are interspersed in the document. Non-biblical warrants for some theological and ethical views are occasionally advanced along with reasonably balanced analyses of economic data. In addition, the paper makes a few positive comments about a market economy.

Drawing selectively on these first three strands of influence, the paper makes a strong appeal to biblical warrants to legitimate church support for specific public policy proposals, to critique market-oriented economies, and to promote the very substantial transformation of the existing form of political economy extant in the United States. Reflecting the focus on orthopraxis, i.e., right conduct, fashionable among liberation theologians, the study paper makes very amorphous distinctions between the community of faith and the community of politics.

In spite of the centrality of political action to promote preferred public policy proposals advanced in the study paper, it does not directly discuss the nature of the state. The paper does, however, appeal frequently to the magistrates and to various international agencies to adopt and to implement policy proposals which it alleges will reduce poverty and economy deprivation.

The study paper does not discuss directly the unique American configuration of economic and political organization called democratic capitalism, an issue which is central to the Pension Boards' statement; but the study paper does express strong criticism of the existing form of political economy in the United States.[7] It calls for economic democracy and a constitutional amendment affirming what it terms "an economic bill of rights." If such proposals were realized, much greater government intervention in the economic sphere than is now the case would occur.

In Christian social ethics one's view of sanctification markedly affects one's view about fitting forms of social organization. People differ in their understandings of the extent to which humans can overcome their propensities toward inordinate self-interest, i.e., their sinfulness, under the conditions of existence, and the effects of finitude, lethargy, sloth, and ignorance. Those locating the primary source of disharmony in social institutions may be more confident about the impact of social reconstruction on human finitude, lethargy, sloth, ignorance, and selfishness than those who locate the primary source of disharmony within the individual person. Those envisaging the persistence of the impact of finitude, lethargy, sloth, ignorance, and inordinate self-interest will be more likely to promote systems devised to provide checks and balances among sometimes competing groups.

The study paper does not explicitly address alternative doctrines of sanctification, but it does envisage the greatly enhanced harmony of life with life among humans through its proposed major transformation of the political economy and the attainment of "economic justice." Because of its relative optimism about the high positive correlation between personal and social transformation, the document has a utopian cast. The new political economy would greatly reduce the impact of finitude, lethargy, sloth, ignorance, and inordinate self-interest in economic and political life.[8]

The study paper strongly urges the adoption of its economic proposals. It claims the proposed transformation of American political economy will enhance the prospects for economic "justice." The document provides little space for those whose prudential judgments about the best means to enhance the being and well being of humankind differ from those proposed in the paper.

Equality is the central principle of justice in this study paper. Because the paper does not consider the relations between love, power, and justice, its nature and limits are not elaborated, and its relation to liberty and to order are not developed. Consequently, the paper has a strongly egalitarian bias.

The paper urges substantial income redistribution between various nation states and suggests that current and proposed international agencies be the primary bodies to facilitate these redistributions. The paper does not consider in any detail either various critiques of the impact of foreign aid on recipient countries or of the international consequences of the emergence of politicized supra-national foreign development agencies and highly politicized third-world countries facilitated by foreign aid.[9]

The text opts for an "intentional fellowship" model of the church rather than a "voluntary church" model. The paper urges strong and inclusive lay and clergy commitment to its understanding of the churches and its view of the way the churches should relate to the public sphere. The "laity" of the voluntary churches are chided for their lack of full total inclusive commitment to the churches, and the New Testament model of the church is lauded. Thus the paper promotes egalitarianism in religious life as well as in economic and political life.

The study paper affirms that in some contexts the church *qua* church and the clergy *qua* clergy should aid and support military action to facilitate social transformation. The paper makes no distinction between the actions of the church *qua* church and its clergy and the political and military actions of lay people. In the context of this discussion, the paper subordinates the principle of order, peace, or harmony — responsibilities of the earthly states — and lifts the principle of equality to a paramount position.

As noted earlier, the study paper's proposed constitutional amendment is probably its most controversial public policy proposal. It is based on the assumption that people have inherent economic rights as well as inherent political rights. The proposed text is: "The right of the people to access to employment, food, shelter, and health care shall not be abridged."[10] The proposal is grounded in the claim that the guarantee for "economic rights is a profoundly biblical concept."

The text notes "an economic bill of rights would bring profound changes to the U.S. economy which cannot be predicted at this time. But standing in the tradition of the prophets and Jesus, we cannot do otherwise than to issue this call."[11]

Assuming the amendment were adopted, the authors of the study paper would ask people in the judicial, legislative, and executive branches of government, lawyers, and labor and business leaders to implement this amendment and to deal with its unanticipated consequences.

Whether one views the proposal to be prophetic, naive, misguided, or irresponsible grandstanding will depend on the evaluative criteria one employs. It would certainly interject lawyers and the courts into the economic sphere to an extent unprecedented in the American experience. It would probably impair economic growth and efficiency, exacerbate inflation, evoke economic shortages, undercut consumer preference as the key factor in allocating resources, heighten conflict within and between various interests groups, and give much more power to politicians than they now possess.

Overall, the paper pays little attention to the likely impact of its policy proposals and the proposed constitutional amendment on economic growth and efficiency.[12] If one thinks economic growth and efficiency are central to the alleviation of poverty and material deprivation, this lacuna is a very serious shortcoming of the paper. Given the high probability that the proposed reorganization of economic institutions and constitutional amendment would impact negatively on economic growth and efficiency, an alternative scenario about the consequences of the proposals for the alleviation of poverty and domestic and international tranquility seems more likely. Declining living standards, economic shortages, high inflation, civil unrest, heightened disharmony within and between interest groups, much more power for politicians, restrictions on liberty, and increased conflict between states seem the more likely outcomes of the paper's proposals.

2. THE PENSION BOARDS' STATEMENT, *THE MARKET SYSTEM AND AMERICAN DEMOCRATIC POLITY: REFLECTIONS IN THE LIGHT OF COVENANTAL TRADITION*

As observed earlier, the Pension Boards Trustees organized a committee whose original charge was to formulate a response to the study paper *Christian Faith and Economic Life*. However, by the time the Pension Boards' committee was organized and functioning, the Pronouncement Committee was already working to formulate its proposed pronouncement, "Christian Faith and Economic Life." Consequently, the Pension Boards' committee decided to develop its own statement on economic life. This 14-page statement, entitled *The Market System and American Democratic Polity: Reflections in the Light of Covenantal Tradition*, is much shorter than the study paper, and it clearly reflects a different view on the Christian faith and economic life than does the study paper.

In its opening paragraphs, this statement notes that the Pension Boards Trustees are offering their prudential judgments on the topic. By appealing to prudential judgments the Pension Boards Trustees recognize that other members of the United Church of Christ congregations may differ in their assessment of the best means to be employed to enhance the spiritual, political, and material well-being of humankind.[13]

To warrant its views, the statement appeals to the quadrilateral sources of authority frequently used by Christian communities: the Bible, tradition, reason, and human experience. In the text these multi-faceted sources of authority interplay with each other, leading to a document somewhat less biblically focused than the study paper and one that is critical of Liberation Theology. In these explications, the text draws substantially from the writings of Max L. Stackhouse.[14] The document underscores the importance of covenant, and it affirms the importance of communities of mutual responsibility.

However, the statement envisages a different structure of political and economic relations in the United States than does the study paper or any of the proposed pronouncements. The statement is more sympathetic to a market economy in the context of a society with a democratic polity than is the study paper or the proposed pronouncements. It affirms that "*continued reliance on the market system as a workable means for Christian Stewardship is not only prudent, it is the system most likely to enable the mission of the church.*"[15]

The general tenor of the statement is reformist, not revolutionary. The key passage affirming this viewpoint reads as follows:

> ... the Trustees of the Pension Boards are convinced that *among the various economic systems available to all nations and investors*, the market system, combined with democratic polity currently in use in the United States, is best able to serve the needs and desires of humanity, including the poor. The market system provides a generally increasing standard of living for most people while operating with minimum restraint on personal liberty and freedom of choice. The democratic polity facilitates income redistribution, limits gross inequality, and provides for persons of special need. Business abuses must be corrected by both the market and the government.[16]

The concluding section refers obliquely to the study paper and anticipates action on the proposed pronouncement on "Christian Faith and Economic Life" at the General Synod. (At the time the Pension Boards' committee was drafting its statement, it did not anticipate two other proposed pronouncements on the Christian faith and economic matters. Given the tenor of the "Christian Faith and Economic Justice" and the "Christian Faith: Economic Life and Justice" proposed pronouncements, the observation would undoubtedly also apply to the other two documents.) The statement says:

> The Pension Boards urge UCC church members and Conferences to consider carefully before resolving to support any kind of economic and political transformation. Care needs to be taken to minimize the coalescence of economic and political power. Any system will be imperfect. We must rely on the morality of people operating within the system most likely to achieve our goals. Multiple centers of initiative are desirable to ward-off excessive power in any single center or person.[17]

Implicit in this statement is an acknowledgement of the continued inordinate self-interest of humans, to be countered by checks and balances and some separation of economic and political power.

The Pension Boards' statement is less egalitarian, more appreciative of the existing interplay between economic institutions and the government in a society with a democratic polity, more sympathetic to a market system, and less utopian than the study paper or any of the proposed pronouncements. Although the statement does not address the problems of the world economy in any detail, it clearly places more reliance on the market system and less reliance on international agency administered foreign aid than does the study paper or any of the proposed pronouncements.

3. THE PROPOSED PRONOUNCEMENT, "CHRISTIAN FAITH AND ECONOMIC LIFE"

The tenor and substance of this 13-page proposed pronouncement and its accompanying 6-page "Proposal for Action" are much like that of the study paper *Christian Faith and Economic Life.* It is somewhat less strident than the study paper, but the proposed pronouncement advances many of the views developed in that paper. Given the close relation between the committee drafting this proposed pronouncement and the committee drafting the study paper, this congruence is scarcely surprising.

This proposed pronouncement, drawing on various strands of liberation theology, proclaims the coming reign of God under the conditions of existence, giving the document a utopian cast. It notes suffering within the human community, cites marks of a just economy, offers an ambiguously negative assessment of the market economy, and calls for much greater state involvement in the economic sphere. Justice is equated with equality, so the document has a rather strong egalitarian bias and proposes substantial income redistribution from so-called first-world to so-called third world countries. It calls on existing and newly created international agencies under the aegis of the United Nations and other international bodies to administer this redistribution.

The United Church Board for World Ministries and the Office for Church in Society, two of the sponsoring bodies, endorsed the proposed constitutional amendment for an economic bill of rights suggested in the *Christian Faith and Economic Life* study paper, broadened to include education. The United Church Board for Homeland Ministries, the third body supporting this proposed pronouncement, rejected the proposal for a constitutional amendment in favor of a pledge to promote the objectives embodied in the proposed constitutional amendment by other political means. The text reads:

> In order to create a country in which the promise of life, liberty, and the pursuit of happiness is fulfilled for each person, we are committed to the passage of a constitutional amendment calling for an economic bill of rights that will provide:
>
> — A guaranteed national minimum income level, ensuring every person access to food, clothing, and shelter;

— A quality health program available to all persons;

— A quality education system that provides to every person nurture, enrichment, and education from infancy to adulthood;

— A right to employment consistent with each person's potential, including a role for the government as employer of last resort;

— A guaranteed right of every person to permanent, affordable, and adequate housing.[18]

In one of the concluding paragraphs of the section dealing with public policy recommendations, the proposed pronouncement suggests that "These proposals suggest a direction for reform of our existing economic system. There are those among us who seek to go beyond reform, desiring new and alternative forms of economic organization."[19] (In fact, if they were adopted, the "reforms" promoted in the proposed pronouncement would dramatically increase government involvement in the economic sphere. They would result in a new form of economic organization.) In the United States, within the two major political parties only a few people in the left wing of the Democratic party would support the self-defined reforms suggested in the proposed pronouncement. Beyond that company, one would have to look at the Socialist party to find significant support for the changes in political economy promoted in the proposed pronouncement.

The proposed pronouncement projects a view of the church and offers a critique of its laity similar to those developed in the study paper, but it is more muted in tone. It accepts the reality of the "voluntary church" which seeks to minister to persons at various levels of spiritual and theological maturity somewhat more gracefully than does the study paper, but it prefers the intentional fellowship model of an inclusive community of very highly committed members.

4. THE PROPOSED PRONOUNCEMENT, "CHRISTIAN FAITH AND ECONOMIC JUSTICE"

Persons representing racial and ethnic special interest groups were dissatisfied with the "Christian Faith and Economic Life" proposed pronouncement, for they felt economic justice rather than economic life was the generic issue to be addressed in a General Synod pronouncement on economic issues. Consequently, persons representing the Commission for Racial Justice and the Council for Racial and Ethnic Ministries drafted a proposed pronouncement which they claimed reflected "a broader perspective, including the concerns of those who primarily do not benefit from the present economic system."[20] The proposed pronouncement was a 9-page document. The accompanying "Proposal for Action" was three pages in length.

The "Christian Faith and Economic Justice" proposed pronouncement makes an even harsher assessment of a market economy than does the "Christian Faith and Economic Life." Drawing on Martin Luther King's address at Riverside Church, New York, in 1967, the proposed pronouncement suggests racism, materialism, and militarism are the underlying motivating factors sustaining the economic system currently extant in the United States. This proposed pronouncement asserts:

> Fundamentally, the capitalist economic system profits from the exploitation, manipulation and monopolization of human as well as financial resources. Inherent in the capitalist economic system is the notion that material profit and the accumulation of capital is more important than an equitable sharing of the wealth of society. This notion contradicts the basic tenets of love and justice as affirmed by the Christian faith. Economic justice in the United States from a Christian perspective would require a transformation of the capitalist economic system.[21]

Although the notion is not explicitly formulated, the principle of justice informing this pronouncement is an equality bordering on egalitarianism. The text does not explicitly discuss the relation of equality to liberty and to order. The proposed pronouncement does not explicitly discuss sanctification, but it does suggest Christians should work "for a nation in which every human being lives fully in dignity, empowerment and joy."[22] Thus, the injustice discerned in the document is contrasted with the hope of the perfect harmony of life with life under the conditions of existence at some future historical time.

The document also sharply criticizes what it terms "the misuse of U.S. military and economic aid in U.S. neo-colonies in Asia, Central America, Africa and the Middle East."[23] It proposes repudiation of third world debt and genuine repentance by the International Monetary Fund and the World Bank "who control the world economic order."[24]

The proposed pronouncement does not address matters of economic growth and efficiency, but it does propose a constitutional amendment embodying an economic bill of right almost identical to the one in the two other proposed pronouncements.

This proposed pronouncement also does not explicitly discuss the nature and authority of the state, but it does appeal to massive state involvement in the economic sphere through its proposed constitutional amendment. Aside from the actions involved in this proposed constitutional amendment, the document does not discuss in detail its view of the nature of the transformed political economy it envisages.

The accompanying "Proposal for Action" calls for a variety of means to work toward "the just transformation of the capitalist economic system into an economic system that fundamentally ensures economic, racial, and social justice and equality in the United States."[25] It also calls for a comparable "just transformation of the global economic order."[26]

The document concludes with the proposal that the Council for Racial and Ethnic Ministries monitor the efforts to implement activities to secure economic justice undertaken by the Commission for Racial Justice, the Office for Church in Society, the United Church Board for Homeland Ministries, the United Church Board for World Ministries, the Office of Communication, and the Office for Church Life and Leadership.

5. THE PROPOSED PRONOUNCEMENT, "CHRISTIAN FAITH: ECONOMIC LIFE AND JUSTICE"

As noted in the preceding chapter, denominational executives responded to the submission of two proposed pronouncements on the Christian faith and economic matters in late March/early June 1989 by engaging in negotiations to resolve the differences between the groups sponsoring the two proposed pronouncements. These negotiations were successful, and just prior to the late June/early July 1989 General Synod meeting, delegates received this new proposed pronouncement. This draft was, in fact, the only one considered at the General Synod.

The "Christian Faith: Economic Life and Justice" proposed pronouncement is longer than either of the others. The "Christian Faith: Economic Life and Justice" text is eighteen pages and the accompanying "Proposal for Action" is eight pages. It draws largely from the "Christian Faith and Economic Life" proposed pronouncement, deleting little from that text. It adds a half-page statement on Christian convictions from the "Christian Faith and Economic Justice" proposed pronouncement, and adds two to three pages of new material, some of which highlights some emphases in the "Christian Faith and Economic Justice" proposed pronouncement. The accompanying "Proposal for Action" incorporated with slight modification six paragraphs of the "Christian Faith and Economic Justice" section on "Directional Statements and Goals" with some material from the "Christian Faith and Economic Life" document.

The proposed pronouncement affirms that God's people have an imperative to achieve economic justice for all people, confesses God's people have been deficient in their efforts, and commits God's people "to transform the structures of church and society by working for economic justice."[27]

Responding to the claims made in the "Christian Faith and Economic Justice" proposed pronouncement, the proposed pronouncement more vigorously critiques the market economy than did the proposed pronouncement, "Christian Faith and Economic Life." It also addresses racism, materialism, and militarism, issues central to "Christian Faith and Economic Justice," but not absent from the "Christian Faith and Economic Life" proposed pronouncement. This new proposed pronouncement's critique of a market economy is not as harsh as is the critique of the proposed pronouncement, "Christian Faith and Economic Justice."

The text draws primarily on biblical warrants for its theological and ethical viewpoint. There is scant appeal to the tradition, human reason and natural law, or general human experience. The hermeneutic associated with the German theologian Jürgen Moltmann, cited in the discussion of the theological sources of the study paper, appears in this version of the text more forcefully than in either of the other two proposed pronouncements.

As noted earlier, this draft included some sections on racism and militarization, incorporating the critiques of American society more forcefully embodied in the "Christian Faith and Economic Justice" proposed pronouncement than in the "Christian Faith and Economic Life" proposed pronouncement.

Aside from new matter on a "Statement of Christian Conviction" on racism and on militarization drawn from the "Christian Faith and Economic Justice" proposed pronouncement, and some rewriting of the biblical, ethical, and theological rationale section to focus even more single-mindedly on the "economic concerns" of God than either of the previous proposed pronouncements, most of the changes involve a reordering and minor rephrasing of paragraphs found in the "Christian Faith and Economic Life" proposed pronouncement.

The accompanying "Proposed Proposal for Action" adds a few new paragraphs, but its overall structures and substance is very similar to the "Christian Faith and Economic Life" proposal for action. Two of the added directional statements summarize well the general tenor of the proposed pronouncement and the proposed proposal for action:

> We establish as a goal the just transformation of the market economy into an economic system that fundamentally ensures economic, racial and social justice and equality in the United States. . . .
>
> We further establish as a goal the just transformation of the global economy into an economic order that fundamentally ensures economic, racial and social justice for all of God's peoples throughout the world . . . [28]

The unequivocal association of racism, militarism, and materialism with capitalism in the "Christian Faith and Economic Justice" proposed pronouncement is deleted in this proposed pronouncement. The statement that some would want to go beyond the transformation of the economic order which appeared in the "Christian Faith and Economic Life" proposed pronouncement is also deleted.

In spite of these deletions and the acknowledgement that in what it terms "the household of God, all current economic systems fall short and are unjust" (Proposed Pronouncement, p. 17), the document offers the same policy proposals as the "Christian Faith and Economic Life" proposed pronouncement, including the same proposed constitutional amendment. In this instance, the Boards of Directors of the United Church Board for

World Ministries, the Commission for Racial Justice, and Office for Church in Society, as well as the Council for Racial and Ethnic Ministries voted for the amendment. As was the case in the proposed pronouncement "Christian Faith and Economic Life," the United Church Board for Homeland Ministries refused to support the proposed constitutional amendment, but committed itself to promoting and establishing the policy objectives in the proposed constitutional amendment.

As was the case with the other two proposed pronouncements, the document has a strongly egalitarian emphasis. Equality, minimally qualified by any forms, biological or social, is the principle of justice. As was the case with the other two proposed pronouncements, the nature of liberty and order and their relations to each other and to equality is not explored in the discussion of justice. Likewise, in spite of the central role the state is called to play in the proposed massive transformation of the economic sphere, its nature and character are not addressed in this proposed pronouncement. It also makes no effort to assess the impact of its proposals on the growth and efficiency of the economy.

This proposed pronouncement also has a utopian cast. It is as optimistic about the positive consequences of its policy proposals and its expectations about the positive consequences of its envisaged radically transformed political economy as are the other two proposed pronouncements. In this regard, it also stands in contrast with those persons who hold inordinate human self-interest is inevitable under the conditions of existence. As noted earlier, different views on sanctification is one of the factors giving rise to contrasting normative views on political economy.

CHAPTER IV

The Adopted Pronouncement, "Christian Faith: Economic Life and Justice"

INTRODUCTION

On the opening evening of the Seventeenth General Synod of the United Church of Christ, a General Synod committee of 38 members selected by lot from General Synod delegates convened for an open hearing on the three proposed pronouncements on the Christian faith and economic matters. This chapter characterizes the process leading to the General Synod adoption of a revised version of the third of these pronouncements, "Christian Faith: Economic Life and Justice." It also considers the General Synod's revisions of the pronouncement.

THE ADOPTION PROCESS

As previously mentioned, the Synod committee assigned to consider the requested proposed pronouncement and the accompanying proposal for action on economic matters were confronted with three proposed pronouncements. The third one, "Christian Faith: Economic Life and Justice," emerged as the text which the committee considered in its deliberations. Parliamentary procedures on this matter were obscure. According to the General Synod Executive Council's "Recommended Standing Rules for the Seventeenth General Synod," copies of Proposed Pronouncements and their accompanying Proposals for Action "must be sent to the Secretary of the Church at least four months before the opening of a General Synod."[1] They will be sent "to the local Churches, Associations, Conferences, and delegates at least three months in advance of a General Synod." In addition, proposals for action will be sent to a proposed initiator(s) three months prior to the General Synod.[2]

As observed earlier, the proposed pronouncement which the committee considered, "Christian Faith: Economic Life and Justice," was never distributed to local churches, associations or conferences. Some of the Synod delegates had received it, others had not. According to a statement distributed to those attending the hearing on the proposed pronouncement(s), "the drafting committee utilized three primary sources in composing `Christian Faith: Economic Life and Justice': the texts of two earlier pronouncements submitted to the Seventeenth General Synod and a revised version of the Christian Faith and Economic Life pronouncement written by M. Douglas Meeks, a member of the drafting committee, which was completed too late to be incorporated."[3]

Because the procedure employed violated those outlined in the "Recommended Standing Rules for the Seventeenth General Synod," a resolution was submitted to the General Synod to give authority to the Synod committee to use the text "Christian Faith: Economic Life and Justice" in its deliberations.

When the open hearing convened, General Synod committee members did not know which of the three documents they were going to consider. Less than half of the committee members were present that evening, so many did not hear the evening's presentations.

According to the established procedure, one person designated by a sponsoring group was given ten minutes to speak in favor of its proposed pronouncement. In fact, all three designated spokespersons supported the third pronouncement, "Christian Faith: Economic Life and Justice." Other persons were allowed to speak for three minutes. One suggested the proposed pronouncement did not deal adequately with ecological issues, one suggested the proposed pronouncement should address the AIDS problem, one suggested a rephrasing and softening of the tone of some of the text dealing with foreign aid, and one urged the deletion of the proposed constitutional amendment on economic rights.

The hearing was then terminated, and the group reconvened two days later. At this session, four persons who had not had time to make three-minute presentations did so. Two suggested the deletion of the proposed constitutional amendment, one suggested more concern about ecological issues, and one suggested the proposed pronouncement be rejected because it promoted a too narrowly-conceived orthopraxis.

Following these presentations, the committee began its deliberations. The members were assigned to small groups to consider assigned paragraphs. The groups would reconvene and report their recommendations. This process was slow and difficult, and the committee members worked long hours to complete their assignment. With the exception of the changes reported in the following section, the revisions were minor. Even had the committee desired to undertake substantial revisions and/or reorganization of the proposed pronouncement and proposal for action, the format and time frame would have made such a project virtually impossible. Once the committee approved the revised document, it was reported to the General Synod at a designated time, discussed briefly, and adopted.

THE SUBSTANCE OF THE DOCUMENT

As noted earlier, the pronouncement "Christian Faith: Economic Life and Justice" was adopted with one major substantive change. The call for a constitutional amendment for an economic bill of rights was deleted, and the wording "we are committed to achieving an economic 'bill of rights' that will provide . . ." was substituted.[4] The United Church Board for Homeland Ministries had recommended this wording.

The document added a brief section on ecumenical initiatives, urging the office of the President [of the UCC] to initiate discussion with the National Conference of Catholic Bishops and "the major Protestant denominations that have written public theologies of economics" to discern the feasibility of the development of an ecumenical document on the topic of economic justice.[5]

In response to requests in the open hearing, a few additional statements on ecology were added. Also, the pronouncement called for the various bodies of the United Church of Christ to continue their advocacy "for the medically indigent and physically disabled due to catastrophic illnesses such as AIDS."[6]

Because the rest of the document is almost identical with the third proposed pronouncement, "Christian Faith: Economic Life and Justice," there is no need to consider it further in this section. A more extended discussion is undertaken subsequently in the section dealing with this author's critical reflections on the substance of the pronouncement.

CHART 2. A COMPARISON OF THE ECONOMICS AND THEOLOGY COVENANT GROUP STUDY PAPER, THE PENSION BOARDS TRUSTEES' STATEMENT, THE THREE PROPOSED PRONOUNCEMENTS, AND THE ADOPTED PRONOUNCEMENT ON SELECTED TOPICS

	Economics and Theology Covenant Group Study Paper (January 1987)	**Pension Boards Trustees' Statement (February 1989)**	**Proposed Pronouncement, "Christian Faith and Economic Life" (circ. about April 1, 1989)**	**Proposed Pronouncement, "Christian Faith and Economic Justice" (circ. about April 1, 1989)**	**Proposed Pronouncement, "Christian Faith: Economic Life and Justice" (circ. June 1989) and the adopted pronouncement, "Christian Faith: Economic Life and Justice (July 1989)***
1. Warrants for Views	Very strong and selective biblical emphasis; other warrants less saliently addressed.	Bible, tradition, reason, and human experience balanced in discussion.	Very similar to Economics and Theology Covenant Group Study Paper.	Very similar to Economics and Theology Covenant Group Study Paper.	Very similar to Economics and Theology Covenant Group Study Paper.
2. View on Political Economy	Transformation promoting much greater involvement of state in economic affairs; political democracy not directly addressed.	Affirms strong support of market system combined with American democratic polity.	Same as Study Paper.	Transformation of capitalist economic system to attain national and international economic justice strongly urged; nature of state not directly dicussed, but it is to facilitate transformation of capitalist economic system into a more "just" system.	Proposal for action calls for transformation of market economy in the U.S. into an economic system insuring economic, racial and social justice and equality; transformation of the global economy into an economic order doing the same for all the people in the world; nature of state not directly discussed, but the government is to effect the domestic transformation and to facilitate, along with other governments and current and newly developed international agencies, the world transformation.

* Only significant change is item 8.

	Economics and Theology Covenant Group Study Paper (January 1987)	**Pension Boards Trustees' Statement (February 1989)**	**Proposed Pronouncement, "Christian Faith and Economic Life" (circ. about April 1, 1989)**	**Proposed Pronouncement, "Christian Faith and Economic Justice" (circ. about April 1, 1989)**	**Proposed Pronouncement, "Christian Faith: Economic Life and Justice" (circ. June 1989) and the adopted pronouncement, "Christian Faith: Economic Life and Justice (July 1989)***
6. View on Human Nature and Social Transformation	New economic democracy and transformed political economy will enhance harmony of life with life and attain greater social justice. Human self-interest will be substantially reduced in the transformed political economy.	Human imperfections suggest checks and balances and some separation of economic and political power.	Same as Study Paper.	Social transformation sought; secure world where all human beings can live fully in dignity, empowerment, and joy for all people.	Same as Study Paper.
7. Role of Government in Economic Sphere	Promote economic democracy, much greater equality, facilitate global income redistribution.	Facilitate income redistribution; limit gross inequality; provide for persons of special needs.	Same as Study Paper.	Promote much greater equality, facilitate global income redistriution and economic transformation.	Same as Study Paper.
8. Proposed Constitutional Amendment on Economic Rights.	Proposed amendment would entail massive involvement of government in economic matters.	No such proposal; views advanced in statement would entail rejection of proposal.	Same as Study Paper. (Not supported by the United Church Board for Homeland Ministries.)	Proposed amendment would entail massive involvement of government in economic matters.	<u>Proposed Pronouncement:</u> Same as Study Paper (not supported by the United Church Board for Homeland Ministries). <u>Adopted Pronounmcement:</u> Constitutional amendment as way to obtain "Economic Bill of Rights" deleted.

CHART 2

	Economics and Theology Covenant Group Study Paper (January 1987)	**Pension Boards Trustees' Statement (February 1989)**	**Proposed Pronouncement, "Christian Faith and Economic Life" (circ. about April 1, 1989)**	**Proposed Pronouncement, "Christian Faith and Economic Justice" (circ. about April 1, 1989)**	**Proposed Pronouncement, "Christian Faith: Economic Life and Justice" (circ. June 1989) and the adopted pronouncement, "Christian Faith: Economic Life and Justice (July 1989)***
3. View of Economic Justice	Principle of equality salient, giving document a strong egalitarian emphasis.	Equality qualified; greater range of economic wealth affirmed; gross inequality to be limited; freedom of choice an important principle.	Same as Study Paper.	Very similar to Economics and Theology Covenant Group Study Paper, but a greater formal emphasis on racial equality as a factor in economic justice.	Very similar to "Christian Faith and Economic Justice" proposed pronouncement.
4. View of Market System	Substantial criticisms of market system to allocate economic resources.	Market system strongly but not unqualifiedly supported.	Slightly more sympathetically treated than study paper but less sympathetically treated than Pension Boards' Statement; less critical than the other proposed pronouncements.	Extremely critical of the market system; racism, materialism, and militarism are products of the existing economic system; capitalist economic system incompatible with Christian faith.	Very critical of market economy, though some strengths are noted; accompanying proposal for action calls for transformation of market economy noted in no. 2 above.
5. Focus on Growth and Efficiency	Little attention paid to impact of policy proposals on economic growth and efficiency.	Growth and efficiency of market a major factor to be considered in policy proposals and in political economy.	Same as Study Paper.	Not considered.	Minimal attention paid to impact of policy proposals and envisaged transformation of market economy on economic growth and efficiency.

	Economics and Theology Covenant Group Study Paper (January 1987)	**Pension Boards Trustees' Statement (February 1989)**	**Proposed Pronouncement, "Christian Faith and Economic Life" (circ. about April 1, 1989)**	**Proposed Pronouncement, "Christian Faith and Economic Justice" (circ. about April 1, 1989)**	**Proposed Pronouncement, "Christian Faith: Economic Life and Justice" (circ. June 1989) and the adopted pronouncement, "Christian Faith: Economic Life and Justice (July 1989)***
11. Role of Church in Support of Military and Para-military Activity to Promote Economic Justice	Condoned in some contexts.	Not addressed.	Not addressed.	Not addressed; highly critical of use of U.S. economic and military involvement in many contexts.	Not addressed.
12. View of the Church	Highly intentional model of church promoted; little room left for contrasting views; New Testament model very important.	Less focus on emphasizing church per se; covenantal relations affirmed; more willing to affirm legitimacy of contrasting views within the UCC.	Intentional model of church promoted, but somewhat more muted critique of voluntary church than the study paper; presses for close rleation of community of faith with a particular agenda for political economy.	View not sharply focused, but pushes for very close identity of community of faith with a particular community of politics.	Same as Proposed Pronouncement, "Christian Faith and Economic Life."

CHART 2

	Economics and Theology Covenant Group Study Paper (January 1987)	**Pension Boards Trustees' Statement (February 1989)**	**Proposed Pronouncement, "Christian Faith and Economic Life" (circ. about April 1, 1989)**	**Proposed Pronouncement, "Christian Faith and Economic Justice" (circ. about April 1, 1989)**	**Proposed Pronouncement, "Christian Faith: Economic Life and Justice" (circ. June 1989) and the adopted pronouncement, "Christian Faith: Economic Life and Justice (July 1989)***
9. Role of International Agencies in Economic Development	Strong support for current and new international agencies to facilitate inter-state income redistribution and economic development in the "third world"; develop new institutions to enhance self-development of poor.	Primary reliance on market system to promote economic growth; no direct addressing of international aid agencies.	Same as Study Paper.	Proposed repudiation of third world debt and genuine repentance by International Monetary Fund and the World Bank "who control the world economic order."	Same as Study Paper.
10. Tolerance for Alternative Views of Political Economy within the United Church of Christ	Very limited; promotes own views very forcefully.	Offers views as "prudential judgments"; contrasting views within UCC should be respected.	Very limited; promotes own views very forcefully; does not note many limits on a market economy which have evolved and continue to evolve in the context of the American experience; little appreciation for American pragmatism; no acknowledgement of possible legitimacy of views of persons who do not concur with some or all of the proposed goals and policy proposals or whose views on means to attain specified goals differ from the pronounement's means.	Promotes own views unequivocally.	Same as Proposed Pronouncement, "Christian Faith and Economic Life."

CHAPTER V

Some Critical Reflections on Process and Substance

INTRODUCTION

In this chapter, the author offers some critical reflections both on the process by which the General Synod's pronouncement on economic matters was developed and also on the substance of the adopted pronouncement. In this author's judgment, the developmental process was flawed, and the adopted pronouncement was too narrowly conceived to warrant its adoption by most of the local congregations in the United Church of Christ. While the author is sympathetic to the pronouncement's desire for minimal levels of food, clothing and shelter for all humankind, his prudential judgment and the judgments of those who developed and adopted this pronouncement as to the best means to attain such objectives — insofar as they can be attained under the conditions of existence —differ substantially. Intertwined with these contrasting prudential judgments are differences about the warrants for one's views, and about one's understanding of justice, sanctification, love-power-justice relations in general and in relation to the several spheres of the human social order, the assessment of the historical situation, the root causes of global economic differences, desirable forms of political economy, and the normative role of religious institutions in the quest for justice.

CRITICAL REFLECTIONS ON THE PROCESS OF PRONOUNCEMENT DEVELOPMENT

In this author's view, United Church of Christ congregations should have substantial latitude to formulate both their beliefs and their practices. Although neither a narrow view of proper belief nor a narrow view of right conduct should be dominant in the United Church of Christ, some local congregations may legitimately entertain such beliefs or practices. Difficulties emerge when protagonists of such narrow views seek legitimation from other parts of the church, particularly the General Synod. Even though it speaks only for itself, the General Synod is the most visible single centering agency in the United Church of Christ. As such, its symbolic activities are more important than those of any other body.

Closely allied with the General Synod are the national agencies and instrumentalities. Members of these ecclesiastical bodies often contribute significant leadership to the deliberations of the General Synod. They also seek legitimation by and funds from the General Synod for projects and causes in which they have special interests. In the last two decades, such causes and interests have greatly proliferated.

The relative direct contribution of the various bodies constituting the United Church of Christ to General Synod deliberations is reflected in data on the number of proposed pronouncements and resolutions submitted to the General Synod by various bodies. In 1989, only three of forty-two proposed resolutions were submitted by local churches. Twenty-three were submitted by conferences and nineteen by national groups. Of the six proposed pronouncements, one was submitted by a group of local churches.

As the data presented earlier on the occupational composition of the committees drafting the various documents on the Christian movement and economic issues revealed, lay people and local clergypersons were very substantially underrepresented in the groups contributing to the adopted pronouncement. Members of various ecclesiastical bureaucracies were overrepresented and were also most influential in shaping the substance and tenor of the adopted pronouncement.

Local church involvement in the pronouncement process was minimal. At a session on the proposed pronouncements at the

1989 meeting of the Illinois Conference, only five of the eighty or so persons present had read either of the two proposed pronouncements mailed to the churches. Three of them were from one congregation.

In late March 1989, the two proposed pronouncements then available (as observed, the adopted pronouncement was not circulated) were mailed to all local churches and to some other parties. The mailing included a request to respond to the proposed pronouncements. The questions for discussing and reporting on each document were prepared by the "recommending" organization. In response to a query by this author, an associate to the Secretary of the denomination reported that, so far as they knew, the instruments were not pre-tested and there were no written documents describing the rationale for the questions. This author had made such an inquiry because the formats employed are not commonly used in social research by people who seek to determine respondents' attitudes on selected topics. The questions had very strong biases in favor of the pronouncements. One would have to make an effort to report negatively. If one were interested in constructing more neutral questionnaire, carefully constructed Likert-type questions would have been preferable to the ones used.

Less than one percent of the local congregations responded to either of the proposed pronouncements. Forty-three local churches responded to the Christian Faith and Economic Justice" proposed pronouncement, and forty-six local churches responded to the "Christian Faith and Economic Life" proposed pronouncement. One special interest group responded to each pronouncement. A majority of the responding churches failed to support either proposed pronouncement. The breakdown of responses, including the special interest group response, in percent, is shown in Table 6.

The low response rate suggests widespread disinterest in national initiatives, a phenomenon also manifest in other areas and in other denominations. The low level of support suggests major problems in consensus formation. Some advocates may not be concerned about this finding. For those desiring broader-based local support for the initiatives of national bodies, these findings are a matter of concern. So far as the author could determine, these responses had no impact on the General Synod's deliberations on the proposed pronouncement.

TABLE 6. RESPONSES FROM LOCAL CHURCHES AND ONE SPECIAL INTEREST GROUP TO FIRST TWO PRONOUNCEMENTS

PROPOSED PRONOUNCEMENT	RESPONSE SUPPORT	OPPOSE	AMBIV.	NO PREF.
Christian Faith and Economic Justice (n = 43)*	44%	30%	14%	12%
Christian Faith and Economic Life (n = 47)	40%	34%	11%	15%

*Only 43 of the 44 responses tabulated.

Source: Letter from the Office of the Secretary, United Church of Christ, dated June 20, 1989.

Because of its multiple centers of initiative, the organizing center of the denomination is not sharply focused. Given the denomination's polity, this situation is inevitable. It is also desirable, for it blunts the temptation for any one body to speak *for* the church.

For a variety of reasons, differing groups and individuals frequently seek official Synod sanction for their views and/or program initiatives. As a result, both narrowly-conceived and more broadly-conceived documents are submitted to the General Synod for review and action. If the denomination really means to affirm theological diversity at its symbolic center, many of the proposals presented to the General Synod should be rejected, for they are either intolerant of alternative beliefs and practices, insensitive to other views, or both.[1]

Because pronouncements and resolutions are composite documents, no one person can claim their authorship. Even in a theological working group where participants share many common presuppositions and prudential judgments, a full consensus is often attained as frequently by exhaustion as by conviction. The situation is exacerbated when participants differ substantially in basic presuppositions and prudential judgments.

In such instances, a consensus cannot be obtained and majority/minority reports are necessary.

A small dedicated group of people largely shaped the tenor and substance of the "Christian Faith: Economic Life and Justice" pronouncement from its conception to its adoption. Others participated in various stages of the process, but a small group — six to at most ten — were largely responsible for its development.[2] Had the process been developed by persons with greater sympathy for American democratic capitalism, the many legitimate concerns addressed in the pronouncement would probably have received a better reception among lay people.

As noted earlier, in the process of the development of the pronouncement which was finally adopted, those few persons who had substantial sympathy for a political economy combining political democracy and a market economy were largely ignored, eliminated from the drafting process, or both.[3]

This selective elimination of more moderate types continued when members of the Commission for Racial Justice and the Council for Racial and Ethnic Ministries responded to the original pronouncement by producing another one. This document, as noted, offered an even harsher assessment of a market economy and of the American experience then the original pronouncement. It was even more adamant in its call for more government intervention in economic life than was the original pronouncement.

The "synthesis," dominated by staff personnel and never submitted to the local churches, was thus a fusion of a document with an ambiguously negative assessment of American democratic capitalism with a document with a strongly negative assessment of America's political economy. Similarly, the synthesis fused a document whose warrants were dominantly biblical with one whose warrants were even more dominantly biblical. It also fused a document maintaining very few distinctions between a community of faith and a community of politics with one maintaining even fewer such distinctions.

The result was a document whose substance is not tempered by many centrist passages. It is reminiscent of documents written by radical transforming sectarian groups in the past — groups accentuating a highly intentional fellowship of persons holding clearly defined beliefs and standing in sharp contrast to the values of the larger society in which the religious institution is set.

Whether such a perspective is fitting for most United Church of Christ congregations is very moot.

CRITICAL REFLECTIONS ON THE SUBSTANCE OF THE ADOPTED PRONOUNCEMENT, "CHRISTIAN FAITH: ECONOMIC LIFE AND JUSTICE"

In this section, the author offers a critique of the substance of the adopted pronouncement informed by an alternative religious social ethic. Although the critique is cast from this author's constructive viewpoint and is informed in its empirical dimension by his prudential judgments, the topics discussed point to persistent issues in religious social ethics to which people offer contrasting interpretations. Consequently, the discussion may be of interest to those not sharing the author's point of view. The topics addressed are the ones cited in Chart 2 to permit comparative assessments of all the relevant documents. Because the topics sometimes overlap, some issues emerge in more than one context.

1. *Warrants for Views Developed*

Within the Christian movement, people differ on the grounds to which they appeal to warrant their views. They also differ in the priority established to the various warrants they offer. In the Protestant tradition, Scripture has often been a primary warrant for one's views. In extreme instances, it has been the sole explicit warrant. (In fact, one's hermeneutical principles always include some implicit metaphysical presuppositions which inform the selective abstractions and interpretations one advances.) In the Catholic Church and in parts of Protestantism, other warrants are often advanced. People have appealed to tradition, reason and human experience to legitimate their views. In some parts of the Christian movement, some segment of the Christian community — designated officials, synods, or some specially designated bodies —have been accorded special authority. Human experience and human reason are always warrants, but their status and their priority depend on one's view of human nature and human reason. (Persons claiming the gift of the Spirit customarily are given greater authority than are persons who have not claimed such gifts.)

The adopted pronouncement places great emphasis on the authority of Scripture — informed by a hermeneutic greatly influenced by the dialectic of negation and by contemporary liberation theology. The pronouncement gives minimal attention to the complexity of the church's teachings on economic life throughout its history, and it makes no effort to ground any of its claims on non-biblical sources. By ignoring the natural law tradition, it needlessly restricts the people to whom its claims might be persuasive. Although the substance is different, in its warrants its claims are as limited as are the claims of biblical fundamentalists.

In this author's judgment, the views of those in the United Church of Christ who place greater priority on tradition, human experience and reason (both "redeemed" and "natural") are inadequately represented in the pronouncement. Denominational pronouncements — if there be such — should be more sensitive to the legitimate theological diversity present in UCC congregations than is evident in this pronouncement.

By failing to incorporate warrants appealing to people outside the Christian movement, the pronouncement needlessly restricts its appeal and accentuates its parochialism. In a pluralistic society and in a world in which the majority of the population is non-Christian, the pronouncement's very strong focus on biblical warrants — even if the hermeneutic used is persuasive to some United Church of Christ members — means it cannot provide a "public theology of economics." A "public theology of economics" must employ warrants which it claims are derivable from general human experience and are not uniquely derived from Christian experience.[4]

In the constructive portions of this chapter, this author does not base his claims on the particularity of the Christian movement. He does acknowledge that his participation in the Christian movement has evoked and heightened his sensitivity to certain dimensions of the common experiences of humankind, but he does not claim they are categorically dependent upon understandings derived from the Christian movement. Consequently, his comments are addressed to Christians and to non-Christians alike.

2. *View on Political Economy*

The failure of the pronouncement to address the nature of the state is one of its most serious deficiencies. Because the state is the only agency which can effect the transformation in the economy called for in the document, the nature and character of the state should be a major topic of the pronouncement.

From this author's perspective, the state is based on social necessity and human rational shaping capacities.[5] Because humans, who find themselves enmeshed in a complex network of social relations, are part of a community, they need to have an organizing center which coordinates some of their activities, provides a basis for defense against internal and external forces, and generally seeks to maintain an earthly peace. Human capacities to formulate general principles and to develop various forms of political organization give rise to rules and regulations of justice and to governments having a monopoly on the legitimate use of force in a given geographical area. Legislative, executive and judicial bodies — sometimes more differentiated than at other times — are incorporated in a state's organizing center.

The economic sphere is based on biological necessity — the basic need for food, clothing and shelter — and human rational shaping capacity. Because social necessity is more inclusive than biological necessity, the state in principle has the right to intervene in the economic sphere. The extent and shape of that intervention are central to the disagreements this author has with the United Church of Christ General Synod's pronouncement on economic life and justice.

Power is the salient component in the political sphere. In the encounter of will with will, the government's right to determine rules and regulations of justice and to use coercion, if necessary, to enforce its rules and regulations of justice all point to the saliency of power in this sphere. At the same time, without the form of justice and the willing participation of most of the people, the state cannot long endure. Thus, justice and love, the secondary and tertiary factors in the political sphere, are necessary requisites for a stable legitimate state.

Among its other functions, the state makes the laws which legitimate economic institutions and define the rules and regulations which apply to their conduct. These rules and regulations of justice provide, as it were, the forms which shape economic life. In this way the dynamic facets of this sphere are set in the context of forms provided by the state. Reciprocity of relations in the economic sphere in some societies — usually those in which technical rationalism (the use of reason to figure out the most efficient way to attain a given end) is highly prized — is rather narrowly defined. Because love is inclusivistic and reciprocal, it cannot be fully manifest in the economic sphere.

Some critics of a market economy undoubtedly long for a social order sustaining full and inclusive human relations in all its spheres. In the economic sphere people must be assessed primarily on the contribution they can make to the tasks that need to be accomplished. Because an economic enterprise must focus on more narrowly defined human relations it cannot deal with its participants in a rich and inclusive way.

In human life in post-traditional societies, the family and other small primary groups, and, in some instances, religious institutions provide the contexts for the development of richer and more inclusive human social relations. The form of the person can be more fully taken into account in these contexts. The intimacy such contexts provide does not assure the realization of wholesome inclusive relations, for primary groups can be very harsh in their treatment of some of their members. State intervention in both economic and familial life may be necessary to protect some people from inhumane treatment.

An awareness of the limits which economic activity sets on human relations will lower one's expectations about the possibilities which can be attained in human relations in the workplace. Even in the most intimate human contexts, human contributions are only partially appropriated by the recipients. In economic life, the contributions and appropriations are more restricted. In fact, only the Divine Life can fully appropriate all which humans have to offer.

In the American experience, the state is a federated form of representative democracy. A written constitution defines complex systems of checks and balances between the legislative, executive and judicial branches of the government, and between the federal government and the state governments. Democracy is the most desirable form of political organization for three reasons: liberty is the constitutive principle of justice; humans have capacities to be concerned with the whole; humans have capacities to be concerned inordinately with themselves. In this discussion, the desirability of a democratic form of government is presupposed.

Although the pronouncement discusses the market economy at great length, it does not adequately address its complex interplay with the government in the United States. It would have been helpful if the pronouncement had distinguished between laissez-faire capitalism, democratic capitalism, democratic socialism, and communism. The distinctions between these various types of political economy are based on the extent to which the state intervenes in the economic sphere and on the form of government extant. While no existing state fits any "type" perfectly, the distinctions are useful to sort out contrasting forms of political economy.

In laissez-faire capitalism, the state places minimal restrictions on property and the functioning of a market economy. In actuality, every state imposes some restrictions on economic activity, but in early nineteenth-century America a market economy existed with very limited government intervention in its operations.

In democratic capitalism, which is the form of political economy extant in the United States today, the government intervenes substantially in the market economy by regulating private capital in numerous ways, by facilitating various forms of income redistribution, and by macro-economic management of the economy through fiscal and monetary policy.

In democratic socialism, the state plays a much greater role in the economic sphere, owning substantial amounts of at least productive capital, such as factories, mines, banking and transportation facilities, and engaging deeply in both the micro and macro management of the economy. As the name suggests, this economic management is combined with a democratic political polity.

In communism, an elitist group manages state-owned property and makes the political decisions about resource allocation. The majority of the population has little or no contribution to either the economic or political decision making.

Because of the acknowledged desirability of democracy and the acknowledged legitimacy of some government intervention in the economic sphere for the sake of justice, the issues discussed here center on the relative merits of democratic capitalism and democratic socialism. While the dividing line is not unequivocally clear, democratic capitalists generally prefer less government involvement in the market economy than do democratic socialists. These contrasting perspectives inform the frequent disagreements this author has with the viewpoints advanced in the pronouncement.

In no nation, and certainly not in the United States, does the government permit the marketplace to function without substantial government intervention. In contemporary America, the government impinges on the market economy through income redistribution schemes, tax policies, regulation of trade and commerce, antitrust legislation, environmental restrictions, safety regulations, pension oversight, minimum wage laws, fiscal and monetary policies, and in numerous other ways. Frequently the pronouncement seems to be attacking a form of laissez-faire capitalism which characterized early nineteenth-century America, but which has long disappeared from the American scene.[6] Because of the very strong emphasis on equality, which will be discussed subsequently, and the minimal attention paid to issues of growth and efficiency, the pronouncement is highly critical of the present form of political economy in the United States.

Because the state, which has a monopoly on the legitimate use of coercion in a society, is the only agency which could implement the objectives which the pronouncement seeks, the pronouncement's proposals would greatly increase its involvement in economic life. In this movement toward an omnicompetent state, political institutions would become increasingly dominant in the American experience. As noted, because the state is not directly addressed in this pronouncement, one cannot be fully clear as to the drafters' explicit views on political economy; but the proposals developed, if adopted, would surely move the society toward democratic socialism. Curiously, even though the pronouncement's drafters are very critical of many state policies, both domestic and foreign, they seem very sanguine about the extension of state involvement in the economic sphere.

Because one's position on a desirable form of political economy is related to one's understanding of justice and one's doctrine of human nature, discussion of this topic is continued subsequently.

3. *View of Economic Justice*

The pronouncement advances equality as *the* principle of justice. Consequently, the document has a strongly egalitarian character. This view of justice also contributes to its harsh advocacy stance, to its minimal attention to the impact of its public policy proposals on economic growth and efficiency, and to its inattention to complex foreign and domestic political issues in its proposals for international development policies and in its critiques of United States foreign policy.

In this author's view, there are three principles of justice. Freedom informed by excellence is the constitutive principle of justice. Equality appropriate to form and peace/order/harmony are the regulative principles of justice. Because the pronouncement makes equality *the* principle of justice and fails to distinguish between constitutive and regulative principles of justice, it is truncated and lacks balance and proportion.

Equality is a mathematical ideal and can never be actualized, for no two entities are exactly equal. Nonetheless, it is an important principle of justice. It does legitimate people's claims for basic minimal levels of food, clothing, shelter, health care and education in a given society. For this reason, this author is sympathetic to some of the policy proposals advanced in the pronouncement. However, if the pronouncement had qualified equality, elaborating its relation to liberty and order and recognizing the limits geography and history place on the principle, it would have offered more persuasive counsel to the churches and to the magistrates.

Equality as a principle of justice needs to be qualified and seen in its complex interrelatedness with liberty and order/peace/harmony, the other two principles of justice. Equality should be qualified by its appropriateness to form. In human affairs, both biological and social factors qualify equality. The limits these qualifications place on equality are equivocal and are subject to debate. Although the limits are somewhat amorphous, they are nonetheless real. Age and sex are universally qualifiers of equality. (In our epoch, the exact limits sex ought to impose on equality are subject to much debate and reinterpretation.) Social function is another limit on equality. In the Middle Ages, for example, equality was set in the context of a social hierarchy, so that different principles of equality applied to people in different social strata. These limitations on equality have been more restricted in the current historical epoch, but they cannot be eliminated. People performing highly prized social functions receive more honor, prestige, and/or remuneration.

Liberty and order/peace/harmony must be considered in order to characterize the complex relations between liberty, the constitutive principles of justice, and equality and order/peace/harmony, the two regulative principles of justice.

Freedom informed by excellence is the constitutive principle of justice because creativity, the ultimate of ultimates at the very base of things, is embodied in the activity of the human organizing center. Excellence points to the way of love, entailing the fitting harmony between the individual and the community. Under the conditions of existence, excellence is never fully attained, and this reality must be addressed in formulating a desirable political economy and in attaining a tolerable balance between the claims of liberty and equality. Because freedom often leads to inequality, and equality often restricts the freedom of at least some people in the community, freedom and equality are not perfectly harmonizable. Further, too restrictive a view of equality blunts novelty and innovation.

The need for the ordering and harmonizing of these partially compatible and partially conflicting principles of justice evokes the second regulative principle of justice — order/peace/harmony. This principle relates most directly to the community and its organizing center, the state; for the state is the agency responsible for harmonizing these mutually necessary but partly contradictory principles of liberty and equality in the rules and regulations of justice applicable to the life of a given living community.

The state must adjudicate between conflicting and competing claims of various groups within the geographical area in which it has a monopoly on the legitimate use of force, and it must defend its interests in the complex interplay of nation-states in the world political arena. The state's leaders must try to assess the likely consequences of various public policies in the quest to attain a tolerable harmony of liberty and equality for its citizens, to promote its interests in international relations, and to maintain an earthly peace.

Because the pronouncement does not cite liberty and order/peace/harmony as principles of justice and has too optimistic a view of human nature, it does not adequately address the inclusive issue of social justice. Neither does it adequately consider the tensions inherent in the state's efforts to harmonize liberty and equality in its rules and regulations of justice, nor does it provide helpful counsel to the magistrates struggling with domestic and international issues in their quest for an earthly peace.

4. *View of the Market System*

Because the pronouncement never defines a market economy *per se*, the lucidity of its discussion is somewhat compromised. In this author's judgment, a market economy possesses the following characteristics: (1) private ownership of the means of production; (2) free access to the market as a consumer, a producer, an investor, or a worker; (3) pursuit of profit as a prime mover for economic activity; and (4) the use of a competitive pricing system to shape the allocation of land, capital and labor and to inform economic choices. In order to function, the system needs the support of a legal order which (a) sustains voluntary and peaceful exchange through the enforcement of contracts and maintenance of a viable monetary system, and (b) seeks in most instances (some "natural" monopolies being the exception) to prevent monopoly practices which disrupt normal supply-demand pricing mechanisms.

In the discussion here, this author will assume the pronouncement's drafters had these characteristics in mind when the text refers to a "market economy."

The pronouncement recognizes some strengths in a market economy, but these strengths are set in the context of an ambivalently negative to a negative assessment of the American experience and a market economy. Even though the pronouncement does not directly attribute the maladies to a market economy, it highlights poverty amid affluence, racism, militarization, economic dislocation, environmental pollution and resource depletion, and powerlessness in its assessment of the American experience in a section entitled "Suffering Within the Household of God." There is no comparable section on "Celebration Within the Household of God." A reading of the text cannot definitively determine whether such an omission is a function of the theological perspective informing the document or is an oversight, but the omission coheres with the pronouncement's assessment of the American experience.

The text cites four strengths of the market economy. First, the market system is more responsive to changes in supply and demand than is centralized planning and is more efficient in allocating resources. Second, "Combined with a democratic political system, the market economy provides enormous freedom of choice for those who are able to participate fully in it. . . . There is some empirical evidence that states with genuine political liberties are market oriented, although the reverse is not true."[7] Third, the market system is usually very productive, for it provides incentives for enhanced productivity and efficiency.[8] Fourth,

> A long history of economic growth and rising standards of living in market economies testify to the advantages of the market system for at least a portion of the population. In the U.S. since World War II, average hourly earnings adjusted for inflation have increased by 60 percent. However, it is also true that since 1970 average hourly earnings have been largely stagnant; increases in household income have occurred only because of an increase in the number of workers in the average household. In Japan and many of the market economies of Europe, capitalism combined with government policies have produced even higher rates of growth and higher and more widely distributed standards of living.[9]

This passage is quoted at length because it illumines an assumption that appears throughout the pronouncement. The last sentence implies capitalism has *not* been combined with government policies in the United States. Beginning in the 1880s, the government has increasingly intervened in the economy. The drafters of the pronouncement are undoubtedly aware of this fact. Why the text does not refer to American democratic capitalism, pointing to the configuration of government intervention to facilitate income redistribution, public policy objectives, and macroeconomic management in a way that preserves a market economy is a puzzle. This author concludes the penchant for democratic socialism among some of the persons drafting the pronouncement led them to interpret the current situation in an ambivalently negative to negative manner.

In this author's judgment, five additional strengths of a market economy should be noted.[10] First, the market system is indifferent to sex, race, religion, or national origin. Unless nonmarket factors intervene, a person who can most effectively perform a given job will be hired. (Biological, social, and personal factors all contribute to differentials in skills among the labor force.) Persons with the resources to purchase desired goods and services will get them. Second, a market system facilitates the proliferation of voluntary associations, publications, artistic endeavors, etc., for people do not have to secure government permission or funding to undertake political, social, economic, cultural, or religious activities. Third, a market system promotes the separation of economic and political power. It promotes multiple centers of initiative and diffusion of power within a society and between various nation-states.[11]

Fourth, the market system limits the development of an "omni-competent state." The state already has many responsibilities in the economic sphere — such as pursuing macroeconomic policy to try to promote stable economic growth, using fiscal policy to facilitate some income redistribution, regulating industry, protecting the environment against industrial pollution, preventing monopoly practices, establishing health and safety standards, enforcing legally binding contracts, coining money, overseeing the financial system, formulating land use regulations, and promoting and funding certain types of research. If the state were to be more deeply embodied in microeconomic matters or were to be directly involved in labor disputes (as an employer), the burdens placed on it would be greatly increased. Every economic issue would become a political issue, and politicians would be blamed for all economic woes befalling the nation or a segment of the nation. Because the state would be one of the parties to labor disputes, it would be very difficult for it to play a mediating role. Such situations would exacerbate social conflict between the state and at least some of its citizens.

Fifth, the market system itself provides a powerful incentive for companies to be concerned with their public image and their acceptance by consumers, for consumers are free to choose alternative suppliers of goods and services. Although it does not eliminate the need for some government oversight and intervention in economic life, this self-regulating "tough ethic" greatly reduces the state's responsibilities.

After citing the four strengths of a market economy, the text turns to a list of the weaknesses of a market economy.[12] It alleges that "the suffering within our own household demonstrates that we face serious economic problems which markets have not alleviated."[13] (The use of the verb "demonstrates" in this context is inappropriate, for the suffering may well have been worse without the workings of a market economy.)

The text then rightly adds that "Not all of these problems are the direct result of the market system. Many of them result from the interactions of our market economy with a host of humanly constructed social and political institutions. Beyond this, Christian faith affirms that there are other than market factors which should motivate our economy, and other claims upon us, including the claims of conscience and of righteousness."[14]

It would seem to this author that the last sentence in this quotation needs much elaboration and clarification. Although claims other than economic ones rightly should contribute to the formulation of public policy, exactly how these other claims "should motivate our economy" is subject to contrasting interpretations. In the main, this author holds public policy initiatives should work *with* market forces rather than *against* them. For example, policies to deter environmental degradation should utilize taxing policies whenever possible to discourage both corporate and individual polluters. Similarly, the negative income tax, which emphasizes individual self-determination, is generally preferable to complex social worker-administered payments for the poor. Political decisions as to the allocation of economic resources are on-going, but these decisions should not try to abrogate market forces.

In spite of this acknowledgment of the complex interplay between economic and noneconomic factors, the text cites seven "weaknesses" of a market economy. First, the market system cannot "guarantee equity of social justice."[15] Second, "market exchange cannot count non-monetary costs and much of vaunted efficiency of markets fails when a full cost-accounting does not occur."[16] Third, the market system "leads not only to gross inequalities of income and wealth, but also to concentration of economic power without public accountability."[17]

Fourth, "A market economy emphasizes individual choice and often ignores the importance of public concerns. . . . The Christian message clearly states that self-interest is not an adequate approach to all economic decisions. There are times when the needs of the larger community, whether that be a family, a church or a nation, must take precedence over self-interest."[18]

Fifth, market systems are "indifferent to what is exchanged, and market systems will respond to military spending as well as to the demand for Barbie dolls. . . . Deciding what should be produced and what should not requires social decision as well as individual decision. Moreover, protecting non-market spheres of life, such as family privacy, requires external restraint."[19]

Sixth, by encouraging mobility and consumption, market systems often corrode community values. "While it is true of other economies, market economies especially encourage false values and priorities. The accumulation of individual wealth and corporate profit is frequently the ultimate measure of success."[20]

Seventh, these six effects are accentuated in the international area, for there are fewer restraints on the market. Greater inequality and unequal economic impact on the global scene by powerful nations characterize the international scene.[21]

The section concludes with the observation, "Given the already alarming inequity of income and wealth and the extraordinary numbers of marginal persons in our society, considerable restructuring must take place even for minimal justice."[22]

With the exception of a few libertarians, people acknowledge most or all of the problems the pronouncement characterizes as weaknesses of a market economy. At the same time, some would think the pronouncement exaggerates the weaknesses and fails to consider trade-offs. In the United States, the Congress, recognizing the fact that the state has a right to intervene in the economic sphere to regulate its activities and to effect income redistribution, has always done so. Since the latter part of the nineteenth century when the excesses of laissez-faire capitalism were plain to almost all, the state has increasingly intervened in the economic sphere. The complex interplay between the state and economic institutions has led to a rather unique configuration called American democratic capitalism. In this system, the state intervenes in the economic sphere, but it does not absorb economic institutions.

Unfortunately, the pronouncement does not note these developments. One may not be satisfied with the scope of these developments, but one may scarcely ignore them.[23] Had they been addressed in the pronouncement, one might be better able to discern the type of "restructuring" which the pronouncement states "must take place." One can infer from other parts of the pronouncement that its drafters want much greater government involvement in economic affairs than is now the case and much greater levels of income redistribution. The more moderate probably want tax increases, a return to more tax brackets, and increased aid to the poor. The more radical seek democratic socialism.

One suspects that the failure to acknowledge the many things the government has done to reduce gross inequality in the United States, to protect the environment, to prevent monopolies, to regulate business, to promote worker safety, to protect the consumer and, in general, to qualify the workings of an unrestrained market system reflected tensions in the drafting committee between those who wanted greater income redistribution with the framework of democratic capitalism and those who wanted to promote democratic socialism. Whatever the reason, the omission is most unfortunate, for it conveys the impression that the state has been utterly indifferent to the shortcomings of the market system. That simply is not the case. For better and for worse, the state has, does, and undoubtedly will continue to qualify the workings of the marketplace.

In some sections, the text expresses a populist bias, urging much more direct citizen participation — particularly among the poor — in public policy formulation. Whether such direct participation is desirable is, of course, highly debatable. Opponents point out that a series of *ad hoc* citizen decisions do not constitute a coherent public policy. The degree of direct citizen determination of public policy issues is a matter on which people may entertain contrasting prudential judgments. The Constitution opted for representative democracy, rather than populist democracy; in this author's judgment, representative democracy is the only workable form in a large, heterogeneous society. The electorate provides a broad direction for the society by electing its leaders and by vigorously promoting their special interests, but elected representatives are responsible for the final decisions.[24]

In listing weaknesses of a market economy the pronouncement critiques both consumer and society preferences for goods and services. The extent to which government action should limit consumer preferences is a matter of continuing debate. Some consumption is limited or prohibited by law in all societies, but the dividing line is never unequivocally clear.

In the example cited in the pronouncement concerning market exchange being indifferent to what is exchanged (which is true), the pronouncement notes that market systems respond to military spending. This is obvious, but the decision *is* a social decision. It cannot be attributed to a market economy. The Soviet Union, which does not have a market economy, allocates more of its GNP to military spending than does the United States.

One of the merits of a market economy is its responsiveness to consumer preference, which is grounded in human freedom. Because consumers frequently make "poor" decisions, market hedonism is often associated with a market economy. Although hedonism is not restricted to market economies, there is no question market hedonism is a major problem in the United States and in other countries with market economies.[25]

Coercion, persuasion, or some combination of the two countervail "poor" consumer choices. The state may try to limit consumer preferences through education, legal restrictions on the production and consumption of certain goods and services, special taxes, or some combination of these. In some instances, legal restraints are successful. In other instances, citizens evade such restrictions, resulting in black markets and the emergence of illegal suppliers.

In helping mold public opinion, religious institutions may contribute to the policy decisions about legal and/or monetary restraints on human consumption and may shape voluntarily the consumption patterns of some people. Due to his conviction that people should have the freedom to be non-free — so long as such non-freedom does not harm others — this author is wary of extensive legal restraints on consumption and production. Some are clearly needed, but the burden of proof must be on those advocating increasing coercive restraints. When such restraints are clearly in the public interest, monetary incentives are generally preferable to direct legal restraints.

While the state can promote education and impose legal restraints in areas of "clear and present danger" (drug abuse, pollution, smoking, AIDS, etc.), other institutions in a society ought to be central in the promotion of "higher values." Families and religious institutions are most important in cultivating people to make excellent consumer choices. The level to which they can elevate human choice voluntarily is unclear. Although some elitists might want the state to coerce people into "higher values," this author is very wary of such proposals.[26]

5. *Focus on Growth and Efficiency*

In keeping with its focus on equality as *the* principle of justice, the pronouncement pays very little attention to the impact of its policy proposals and its envisaged transformation of the market economy on growth and efficiency.[27] It does promote economic democracy, which would extend decision-making in an egalitarian horizontal manner. It also laments the disruption to personal and community life caused by rapid social change and excessive horizontal and vertical social mobility, but it does not explicitly suggest how such disruptions are to be restricted.

It is the author's view that unlimited economic growth and efficiency are not the goal of economic life or of a good society, but economic growth and efficiency are important. People derive aesthetic satisfaction from participating in an organization that is well run and not wasteful of time and resources. Nonetheless, public policies may restrict economic growth and efficiency, for one must strive for a proper balance between economic growth and efficiency and the humane treatment of employees, the protection of the environment, and the promotion of noneconomic values.[28] Because of its one-sidedness, the pronouncement provides little guidance on this complex issue.

Given the persistence of human self-interest, the majority of voters are unlikely to support voluntarily income redistribution schemes that would reduce their own standards of living. Economic stagnation or decline would most likely exacerbate conflicts within and between groups and result in declining living standards for all. Consequently, unless the economy maintains a "reasonable" rate of growth, the prospects for the peaceful economic betterment of the disadvantaged are minimal. If this prudential judgment is correct — and this author believes it is — one must support public policies and a form of political economy that show reasonable prospects of promoting some economic growth and pay substantial attention to economic efficiency.

It is revealing that none of the policy proposals advanced in the pronouncement promoted capital investment directly or addressed the need for economic incentives to promote human efforts. One proposal, the call for "a quality education system that provides to every person nurture, enrichment and education from infancy to adult," would result in increased investment in human capital.[29] If the call to members "to adopt a personal and family lifestyle consistent with life in the household of God and God's creatures" resulted in reduced consumption and increased savings, this proposal would also promote capital investment.[30] The massive state intervention in the economic sphere advanced and/or implied by the pronouncement would likely countervail the impact of these proposals, for the levels of suggested state intervention in the economic sphere and of global income redistribution would retard economic growth and efficiency.

The pronouncement properly notes the need for an improved availability of food, clothing, housing, health care, and education for some segments of the population in the United States and, on a broader scale, for people in the Third World. In the American context, continued immigration from poverty-stricken countries in Latin America, an upward revision of the poverty level depending upon improved general economic conditions, and the human misallocation of individual and family resources assure a continuing poverty problem for the foreseeable future.

In many parts of Asia, Africa and Latin America, conditions are obviously more extreme. Unless capital investment is encouraged more strongly than is done in the pronouncement, the prospects for alleviating poverty in much of Asia, Africa and Latin America are dim. In any event, external assistance cannot facilitate economic growth in less developed areas of the world unless these areas are willing to rely very substantially on the market economy.

In sum, it seems highly likely that if the pronouncement's proposals were adopted, they would result in economic stagnation at best and economic decline at worst. At the minimum, the pronouncement should have noted the tensions in some areas between equality and efficiency, recognized the need to encourage increased capital investment, considered the need for economic incentives to encourage people to work beyond a minimal level, and addressed the issue of risk, profit and uncertainty.

If this author's prudential judgments as to the impact of the pronouncement's policy proposals on growth and efficiency are correct, persons seeking guidance as to feasible ways to alleviate poverty and to facilitate a tolerable balance of liberty and equality appropriate to form under the conditions of existence will have to draw on sources other than this General Synod pronouncement.

6. *View of Human Nature and Social Transformation*

While recognizing the persistence of human sinfulness, the pronouncement does envisage an earthly future in which "the rule of justice prevails in the human household."[31] Because equality is the principle of justice in the pronouncement, the "rule of justice . . . in the human household" would result in an egalitarian human household. The pronouncement is equivocal in its views on the persistence of sinfulness among the sanctified. In one passage the text notes that "we are called to live out" the Great Commandment.[32] It then continues: "As we confess and repent, we declare our intention to work and struggle for a nation and a world in which every human being is empowered to live life fully, joyfully, and in dignity."[33] Had the drafters held that inordinate self-interest needs to be taken into account perennially in human life, they would have been much less sanguine about their proposals to give more power to politicians and to persons associated with international agencies. They would also have been less optimistic about the contribution of their proposed transformation of the political economy to the quest for justice. Had they given more recognition to the disharmonies which finitude, lethargy, sloth, ignorance, and inordinate self-interest evoke in human life, the pronouncement's drafters would have been led to a quest for forms of human social organization that both enhance human propensities to be concerned for the whole and also countervail human propensities to be concerned inordinately with the self. Because the pronouncement inadequately recognizes these dual tendencies in human beings, it fails to address the need for the separation of power between political and economic institutions. The pronouncement places too much confidence in politicians to effect and to sustain the radical transformations of the political economy for which it calls. It also underestimates the need for incentives for people to work. Consequently, it places insufficient stress on the need for humans to bear at least some of the consequences for bad economic decisions and to reap at least some of the benefits for good economic decisions.

Although one cannot discern clearly the substance of all the "structural reforms" called for in the pronouncement, a reader would surely observe leanings in the direction of democratic socialism. As frequently observed, in this author's judgment democratic capitalism offers greater promise to alleviate poverty and to enhance human self-determination than do other forms of political economy. It also sustains the checks and balances so important in facilitating a democratic polity and in promoting reasonable efficiency and growth in economic institutions.

7. Role of the Government in the Economy[34]

As already discussed, the pronouncement envisages much greater involvement of the government in the economic sphere than is currently the case. The proposed constitutional amendment promoting an "economic bill of rights," rejected by General Synod delegates, would have entailed immense and unanticipatable new government involvement in economic life. Although the pronouncement does not specify an allowable range of economic inequality, it clearly envisages much greater economic equality than is presently the case. It also promotes an unspecified global income redistribution and economic transformation, for which the government would have to provide the funds by increasing taxes. To facilitate this income redistribution, the pronouncement calls for new international agencies to supplement the work of existing ones.

In this author's judgment, the government should facilitate income redistribution to limit gross inequality and to provide assistance for persons with special needs. Because he qualifies the principle of equality, sets it in relation to liberty and order, is concerned about incentives, is more sanguine about private concentrations of wealth, is skeptical about the value of many of the funds spent on foreign aid, and wants to maintain a vigorous private economic sector, it is almost certain that this author would not support as high a level of transfer payments as would the drafters of the pronouncement. Because the drafters of the pronouncement did not richly detail the means to be employed to effect their policy objectives, one cannot be certain about the likely differences in policy proposals between them and this author. This author would probably more frequently support efforts to alleviate poverty that work *with* market forces rather than *against* them. He would probably be more willing to support proposals to strengthen the private sector and to provide financial incentive for the pursuit of excellence and the development of human potential than would the drafters of the pronouncement.

One area of likely agreement between this author and the drafters of the pronouncement would be the allocation of increased resources for education. The pronouncement's rather humanistic vision of quality education is commendable, but it needs to be supplemented by a focus on technical competence. It is unfortunate that the pronouncement did not refer to "human capital," for good education constitutes such an investment.[35] Such an approach would have broadened support for its proposal in this area, for education is critical to economic growth and efficiency. It also is central to the reduction of gross inequality in the social order.

8. *Proposed Constitutional Amendment on Economic Rights*

As noted, the General Synod rejected the proposed constitutional amendment encompassing an economic bill of rights. The adopted pronouncement affirmed the pledge to work for a guaranteed national minimum income level, a quality medical program available to all persons, a quality education, a right to employment consistent with one's potential, and a guaranteed right to decent housing.

Because the pronouncement does not specify in detail either the levels desired or the means to attain them, one can only conjecture about the drafters' view of the implications of the pledge for public policy.

Given the tenor of the document, one can reasonably infer that the drafters envisage more government intervention in the economic order. Whether such intervention is to work with or against market forces is unclear. Given the general orientation of the pronouncement, the drafters probably envisage more governmental paternalism, lawsuits, and special privileges to move toward the unspecified acceptable levels of equality.

Few would deny the desirability of adequate incomes, quality health programs, good education, good employment and decent housing for all human beings. In seeking to enhance human life, one must consider the most appropriate means to use consistent with the promotion of liberty, consumer preferences, order, and economic growth and efficiency.

Judged by these criteria, the pronouncement's goals seem fuzzy and the means to attain them seem obscure. The attempt to specify national levels of decency and to mandate "employment consistent with one's potential" seem suspect. In addition, the pronouncement does not address the propensity of many people — if not all — to mis-allocate their resources and to display sloth and lethargy.

At the same time, the pronouncement's efforts to draw attention to these human needs is commendable. People in the public and private sectors will probably continue their pragmatic and experimental efforts to enhance the quality of human life. In so doing, they will have to pay more attention to liberty, order, and economic growth and efficiency than the pronouncement does.

9. *Role of International Agencies in Economic Development*

The pronouncement calls for the strengthening of current international agencies or the establishment of new ones to address continuing and emerging economic problems in global economic development, decision-making power for poorer nations, debt restructuring, and greater regulation of transnational corporations. The pronouncement does not make detailed proposals, but it places great emphasis on international agencies. In this author's judgment, the pronouncement places too much reliance on international agencies and pays inadequate attention to the role of nation-states in international affairs. The pronouncement takes this approach because it does not deal directly with the nature of power and its relation to love and justice.

In political life, power is the leading component in the power-justice-love triad. In the domestic realm, where it has a monopoly on the legitimate use of force to carry out its will, a state cannot long endure without embodying forms of justice and evoking the empathetic participation of most of its members. Thus, justice is the secondary component and love is the tertiary component. Power itself is always interactive or reciprocal, never linear, but some people and groups have more power to influence actions than do others.

Power is especially salient in international affairs because no transnational agency can enforce its laws effectively and people share so few transnational symbols. Given this situation, which seems likely to persist in the foreseeable future, nations are very reluctant to relinquish even part of their sovereignty to international bodies. The pronouncement's failure to address this reality and its implications for international relations makes its comments in this area largely irrelevant.

Due to these realities, one should be alert to the ambiguity and tenuousness of international agencies in the relations between nations. One should also encourage appropriate bilateral and multilateral national accords and, in many instances, place less reliance on international agencies.

The pronouncement has no positive things to say about the role of transnational corporations in economic development. It also fails to call for greater reliance on the private sector and on market economies in less developed countries.[36]

These lacuna are especially puzzling in the light of the recent efforts of Russia, China, and eastern European countries to move toward market economies. Inefficiency, lack of economic growth, and pervasive government officialdom are the hallmarks of these political economies.[37]

10. *Tolerance for Alternative Views of Political Economy Within the United Church of Christ*

Although the pronouncement recognizes "there is no clear or easy way to move from biblical and theological mandates to particular policy recommendations,"[38] it expresses little tolerance for the views of UCC members whose understanding of justice and/or whose prudential judgments on the most effective means to move toward greater "economic justice" differ from those of its drafters. It fails to make adequate distinctions between the community of faith and the community of politics.

The pronouncement does not elaborate in detail the nature of the "considerable restructuring" of the political economy which must take place, but it does reject the notion that "charity and economic growth will ameliorate suffering and growth."[39] The proposed constitutional amendment on economic rights, rejected by the General Synod, is strong evidence that its drafters envisage much greater governmental involvement in the economic sphere than is now the case. Whether a further extension of federal paternalism, special treatment and lawsuits constitutes a better way to alleviate poverty than rightly-conceived charity and economic growth is a moot question.

The pronouncement does not strongly support government monetary and fiscal policy designed to promote economic growth and efficiency to alleviate poverty. It is strongly biased in favor of income redistribution schemes and governmental intervention. Persons sympathetic with the views of the left wing of the Democratic party and the Socialist party are likely to be within the drafters' community of politics; members of the Republican party and moderate Democrats are likely to be outside of it.

In addition to its failure to allow sufficient room for differing prudential judgments on matters of political economy and public policy within the community of faith, the pronouncement assumes the unquestioned validity of its "biblical and theological" mandates. In a denomination which has prized theological diversity, this affirmation is surprising. It assumes that its hermeneutics is *the* denominational viewpoint. In so doing, the pronouncement substitutes a narrowly-conceived orthopraxis, i.e., right conduct, for a narrowly-conceived orthodoxy, i.e., right belief.[40]

In this author's view, the failure of the pronouncement to acknowledge the legitimacy within the United Church of Christ of alternative biblical and theological mandates, alternative understandings of justice, alternative views of a desirable political economy, and alternative prudential judgments as to the best means to alleviate poverty is most serious. As one who has prized his association with a denomination which has valued theological diversity, he finds this insensitivity most embarrassing and most unfortunate.

Because the General Synod speaks only for itself, local congregations and church members may ignore or reject this pronouncement without violation of conscience and remain within the broad community of faith. Unfortunately, persons in the national bodies sponsoring this pronouncement will probably use it to legitimate the interpretations they advance and the public policy objectives they pursue.

11. Role of the Church in Support of Military and Paramilitary Activity to Promote Economic Justice

The pronouncement did not discuss direct church support of military and paramilitary activity in some contexts to promote economic justice. Of the various documents, only the study paper supported such activity in some contexts.

There is no way to know whether conviction or oversight contributed to this omission. However, in this author's view, it should be omitted on principle, for religious institutions should not directly support military and paramilitary activity in any context to promote economic justice. This judgment is grounded on the priority of love in the love-power-justice triad in the religious sphere. In this sphere, love is the leading component, for religious institutions should bear primary witness to God's love for the world. God's love is persuasive and not coercive; God is supremely sensitive to the needs of emerging creatures and supremely responsive to that which they offer to the Divine Life. From the creatures' point of view, justice is the secondary component and power is the tertiary component in God-world relations. Because of their special symbolic role in religious communities, clergypersons should be very wary about engaging in any direct involvement in military action, in which coercion dominates, and should be wary as well of indirect involvement in it.

In the political sphere, as noted earlier, power is the leading component, justice is secondary, and love is tertiary. Sometimes coercive power must be exercised for the sake of justice and of love, so lay people may legitimately, in some contexts, support military action to promote justice and love. Depending on the context, the action may be to support an existing state or to overthrow an existing one. Because of the role of the state in the promotion of earthly peace, order and harmony, the revolutionary must have an extremely strong case to legitimate his or her actions. In some circumstances he or she may make a persuasive case, but the burden of proof is clearly upon the revolutionary.

12. Views of the Church

The pronouncement promotes a highly intentional model of the church. Its drafters are very confident that its biblical and theological mandates and its view of their implications for "economic justice" ought to be *the* theological and social ethical perspective informing the churches comprising the United Church of Christ. They think UCC members should have a strong commitment to the views it elaborates. The pronouncement displays little sensitivity to the UCC's congregational polity, to its inclusion of churches with a diversity of beliefs and practices within its associations and conferences, and to the legitimacy of alternative biblical and theological mandates and their implications for "economic justice" and political economy.

The pronouncement encourages the bodies sponsoring it, i.e., the Office for Church in Society, the United Church Board for World Ministries, the United Church Board for Homeland Ministries, the Commission for Racial Justice, and the Council for Racial and Ethnic Ministries, "to appoint a task force to expand this pronouncement into a fuller study resource, similar to *A Just Peace Church*, and, in cooperation with Conferences and Associations, to conduct a church-wide study process."[41]

As resource pieces, the study paper and the pronouncement, the documents currently available, are too narrowly conceived, too doctrinaire, and too limited in scope to facilitate thoughtful discussion of very complex issues. Unless substantial changes in the sponsoring groups' basic approach to education takes place, the projected document will suffer the same limitations as the current ones.

Local clergypersons seeking to provide their laypeople with a balanced perspective on religious social ethics and to explore alternative approaches to very complex public policy issues in economic life would have to draw on other resources. Many are already available. Local congregations, associations, conferences, and people outside denominational agencies and instrumentalities could develop supplemental resource materials.

This suggested approach presupposes the legitimacy of varying levels of commitment to particular beliefs and practices within and between churches in the United Church of Christ. It coheres with the author's basic disagreement with the documents thus far developed by the sponsoring agencies: their unwillingness to acknowledge the legitimacy of contrasting theological interpretations and differing prudential judgments among members and churches on matters of economic justice and political economy.

In this author's judgment, the denomination would be better served if people responsible for developing denominationally sponsored educational resources sought to produce materials reflecting a genuine plurality of theological approaches to social ethics. The material should illumine different approaches to public policy issues and different views of relations between the community of faith and the community of politics. It should help people make up their own minds; it should not try to indoctrinate them with the point of view of a segment of people within this complex and variegated denomination. To facilitate this process, the material should consist of powerful and persuasive readings on religious social ethics and economic life drawn from authors holding contrasting interpretations.

In the judgment of this author, a book of carefully selected readings representing contrasting interpretations of the Christian faith and economic life would be a far better educational document than a task force developed "fuller study resource." Because some of the readings would include the positions of persons supporting consequentialist social ethics, which entail the requirement that a person must explore the likely consequences of public policy proposals in making a recommendation, readings should include essays by human scientists as well as religious social ethicists. In addition, representative major social philosophers who have informed the thinking of religious social ethicists should be included.

An inclusive book of representative readings would decrease the likelihood of reducing education to indoctrination. Such an approach might not produce many zealots for a particular point of view, but it would enhance the quality of the decisions people make. Most importantly, it would honor the fact that human beings are meaning-seeking, meaning-positing creatures. Human freedom is enhanced when people are encouraged to make up their own minds on theological and moral issues. One may disagree with the decisions some people make, but one may rejoice that the decision-making context encouraged them to undertake a free and open exploration of a variety of alternatives before coming to their decisions. The liberal heritage embodied in facets of the United Church of Christ and the congregational polity of the denomination both encourage such a framework for education and for decision-making.

The denomination needs to cultivate ways to permit members to express their social concerns without forcing them to join a particular community of politics when they become members of the community of faith. Some highly socially active local congregations require such commitments — at least implicitly. If a genuine consensus on selected public policy issues exists in a local congregation, such a convergence should be honored — provided those congregations do not seek to impose their view on *all* congregations or national bodies.

Because of the constitutional autonomy granted to local churches, associations, conferences, national bodies, and the General Synod within their own spheres, no body can impose its views on another. In this author's judgment, this arrangement is so desirable that some of the negative consequences of the polity must be endured for the sake of this general principle. When spokespersons for national agencies address public policy issues, they should very consciously note that because of the denomination's polity, they speak only for the group or groups they represent and not for the churches. Local congregations do have the right to determine their benevolence giving. If other bodies determine to engage in program emphases with which many lay people disagree, they can respond by refusing to fund such projects. A greater use of designated giving would permit lay people to have more voice in shaping denomination activities. Such designated giving for specified public policy endeavors and for specified national bodies would constitute a step in the direction of separating more clearly the community of faith from the community of politics. If designated giving were widespread, national and conference bodies would have to build a strong case for their proposed activities. Lay people in agreement could give to the projected project and lay people in disagreement could withhold their support.

Various agencies and program emphases might receive more or less support under such an arrangement. In any event, people would know they were funding programs and projects which they could, in conscience, support as legitimate expressions of their religious convictions. People could refrain from funding programs and projects which, in conscience, they could not support. In this way, the distinction between one's community of faith and one's community of politics could be illustrated.

The pronouncement fails to encourage active lay participation in secular voluntary associations and special interest groups promoting social justice and human rights. This omission is unfortunate, for by focusing on *church* action, the pronouncement circumscribes too narrowly lay activity in the public sphere.[42] One can only speculate as to the reasons for devoting so little attention to the issue of citizen participation in secular bodies. Persons who are sensitive to the normative desirability of maintaining some distinctions between the community of faith and the community of politics are more likely to address this question than are persons who are willing to identify their community of faith with their community of politics. Perhaps the drafters of the pronouncement, being relatively insensitive to the need for such distinctions, did not address this question. (As observed previously, liberation theologians, strongly emphasizing praxis, are very prone to identify the community of faith with a particular community of politics. Some of the drafters were much influenced by this movement in contemporary theology.)

If one holds that concerned Christians may legitimately differ on desirable forms of political economy and may entertain differing prudential judgments as to the best means to facilitate the quest for social justice and human rights, churches should encourage their members to support and to participate in the special interest groups and voluntary associations which the members think are working for goals they can affirm with theological integrity. By expressing their social concerns through secular agencies, people in the same community of faith may both maintain legitimate distinctions between their community of faith and the community of politics and also have their faith inform their politics.

A CONCLUDING NOTE

The evolution of the United Church of Christ General Synod's pronouncement on the Christian faith and economic issues has been traced from its initiating phase in 1980 to its adoption at the Seventeenth General Synod in 1989. Because of its congregational polity and its consequent lack of any definitively authoritative body of doctrine, the development of a particular document depends upon the commitment of a company of people who want to develop it.

The advocacy stances of many national agencies and the various commissions and special interest groups created by various General Synods provided the context out of which this pronouncement emerged. Within this ethos, three or four deeply committed persons not affiliated with national bodies and three or four staff people assigned by sponsoring bodies to work on this project shaped the development of this pronouncement.

The views of particular participants, set in the framework of the complex interaction between more transient committee members, the central participants, the decisions of two bodies to formulate different proposed pronouncements and of one body to formulate a statement of the Christian faith and economic matters, contributed to the development of an adopted pronouncement which is very insensitive to alternative interpretations of the Christian movement and economic matters and which fails to acknowledge the legitimacy of contrasting prudential judgments about the best means to alleviate poverty. The fact that the delegates to the General Synod did not raise critical questions about this approach is disturbing.

The pronouncement process was flawed, for the most numerous constituency in the denomination, lay people employed in the private sector and in the government, were seriously underrepresented in the various committees. Had they had fair representation, there is every reason to believe a more balanced document would have emerged. (Whether it would have been adopted is another question, for synod delegates often do not reflect the broad range of views manifest in local UCC congregations.)

The process was further flawed by the very poor feedback from local congregations. Indifference, insufficient time to respond, and poorly designed feedback instruments all contributed to very low local church involvement in the pronouncement process. Finally, the final form of the proposed pronouncement was not submitted to the local churches for their consideration. In the author's judgment, this oversight is a result of the fact that many denominational leaders are insensitive to the role local churches ought to play in denominational affairs.

While there is no constitutional mandate for national bodies or General Synod delegates to take the views of local churches into account, it would seem very wise to do so. Unless local congregations have some contribution to make to the pronouncement process, they are unlikely to pay much attention to those that are adopted.

This author has detailed his disagreements with the substance of the pronouncement. He is confident that some of his disagreements are shared by others in the denomination. However, his fundamental disagreement is at a more basic level. He thinks the drafters of the pronouncement should have been willing to acknowledge the legitimacy of contrasting theological interpretations and differing prudential judgments on matters of economic justice and political economy within and between the congregations of the United Church of Christ.

At this level, the disagreement may be unresolvable. This author is, at the foundational level, committed to the legitimacy of responsible theological pluralism and theological diversity within the denomination. No fallible forms can fully convey the depth of feeling and meaning embodied in the Christian movement and sustained within the United Church of Christ. Alternative abstractions from the matrix of this rich experience both clarify and obscure the nature of things. They are complimentary and ought to co-exist within the life of the denomination.

Those who want the churches of the denomination to affirm *their* interpretation must be uneasy about this view of the legitimacy of theological diversity and theological pluralism. This author is fully prepared to affirm the legitimacy of the inclusion in the denomination of persons and congregations that espouse what he has termed "a narrowly-conceived orthodoxy" or "a narrowly-conceived orthopraxis," so long as they do not impose their beliefs or practices upon those who reject them. Because, in his judgment, the pronouncement embodies "a narrowly-conceived orthopraxis," this author regrets its adoption by the General Synod. By the same token, he would not want the General Synod to incorporate the constructive views expressed here to critique the adopted pronouncement in an alternative pronouncement. In this author's judgment, General Synods should adopt many fewer pronouncements and resolutions.

As the most important single symbolic component in the United Church of Christ, the General Synod should be especially sensitive to the legitimacy of diversity of thought and action and to the legitimacy of some distinctions between the community of faith and the community of politics in the United Church of Christ. If the General Synod chooses to act in sectarian ways, then local congregations, conferences and associations may choose to countervail its actions.

If this pronouncement evokes thought and discussion within the denomination on the crucial issues it addresses, it may be of some use. Even so, because of its lack of balance and proportion it may do more harm than good. Some zealots may uncritically affirm it, but many UCC members will be unimpressed with it.

Because many who do not understand the polity of the United Church of Christ will think that it represents the denomination's teachings on the Christian faith and economic life, its presence in our midst is unfortunate. If the General Synod wanted to produce a public theology of economics (which this author thinks it should not do), it could have done better than it has.

NOTES

INTRODUCTION

1. Quoted in Audrey Chapman Smock, editor, *Christian Faith and Economic Life* (New York: Hunger Action Office, United Church Board for World Ministries, 1987), p. iii.
2. *General Synod Handbook: Seventeenth General Synod, United Church of Christ, June 29-July 4, 1989* (no editor, place of publication or date cited; distributed to General Synod delegates in April 1989), p. 16.
3. Smock, ed., *Christian Faith and Economic Life*, p. iii.
4. The page references to *The Market System and American Democratic Polity* are the pages in this volume. The page references to the other two documents are the pages of the original documents which appear at the bottom of the pages in the appendix.

CHAPTER I

1. For a more extended discussion of the polity of the United Church of Christ and its impact on denomination activities, see W. Widick Schroeder, "People, Policies, Politics and Programs: The Adoption and Implementation of Denominational Priorities in the United Church of Christ," in *The United Church of Christ: Studies in Identity and Polity*, ed. Dorothy C. Bass and Kenneth B. Smith (Chicago: Exploration Press, 1987), pp. 75-82.

CHAPTER II

1. Smock, op. cit., p. iii. The co-chairs of this committee, Douglas Meeks, Professor of Systematic Theology and Philosophy, Eden Theological Seminary, and James Weaver, Professor of Economics, American University, are both very critical of American democratic capitalism. Meeks promotes policies leading toward democratic

socialism. A memo by Weaver promoting a proposed constitutional amendment advancing an "Economic Bill of Rights" was circulated to the General Synod committee deliberating on the proposed pronouncement. This amendment was deleted in the adopted pronouncement. It is discussed at length in the body of the study.

2. Ibid., p. iii.
3. Ibid., p. iii.
4. In fact, only a very small percentage of white middle and upper class Americans would support the interpretations advanced or the proposals developed in this "Christian Faith and Economic Life" proposed pronouncement. Viewed from an outside perspective, the disagreements constituted a modest family quarrel. However, as noted in the text, the controversy did interject minority spokespeople more forcefully into the whole pronouncement process. In interpreting the pronouncement purporting to be a synthesis of these two pronouncements to the General Synod Committee dealing with all three pronouncements, the chairperson of the original Pronouncement Committee, one of two non-staff people involved in drafting the third pronouncement, commented that the two earlier proposed pronouncements differed more in style than in substance.
5. Letter to the author, dated May 4, 1989.
6. The 1989 budgets for the bodies endorsing the proposed pronouncement are: United Church Board for Homeland Ministries, $13,575,900; United Church Board for World Ministries, $13,462,306; Commission for Racial Justice, $998,548; Office for Church in Society, $819,880; Council of Racial and Ethnic Ministries, $12,740. (Source: *United Church News*, June 1989, p. 9.)
7. In 1988 racial/ethnic minority groups constituted 5.9 percent of the total UCC membership of 1.66 million. The percent of the various racial/ethnic minority groups is as follows: African-American, 3.7 percent; Asian-Americans and Pacific Islanders, 1.5 percent; Hispanics, 0.6 percent; and Native Americans, 0.1 percent. Source: *Keeping You Posted*, vol. 24, no. 5 (May 1989), p. 1.

CHAPTER III

1. See, for example, Jürgen Moltmann, *The Church in the Power of the Spirit* (London: SCM Press, 1977); *The Crucified God* (New York: Harper and Row, 1974); *The Gospel of Liberation*, trans. H. Wayne Pirkin (Waco, Tex.: Word Books, 1973); *Hope and Planning* (New York: Harper and Row, 1971); *On Human Dignity: Political Theology*

and Ethics, trans. with intro. M. Douglas Meeks (Philadelphia: Fortress Press, 1984); *The Open Church: Invitation to a Messianic Lifestyle*, trans. with intro. M. Douglas Meeks (London: SCM Press, 1978); *The Power of the Powerless*, trans. Margaret Kohl (San Francisco: Harper and Row, 1983); *Religion, Revolution, and the Future*, trans. M. Douglas Meeks (New York: Charles Scribner's Sons, 1969); *Theology of Hope* (New York: Harper and Row, 1967).

2. Meeks has recently published a volume focused on the Christian faith and economic matters. Not surprisingly, it embodies many of the motifs appearing in the study guide, one of the proposed pronouncements, and the adopted pronouncement. See Douglas Meeks, *God the Economist: The Doctrine of God and Political Economy* (Minneapolis: Fortress Press, 1989).
3. Gustavo Gutiérrez is perhaps the best known Latin American theologian employing Marxist modes of social analysis. See, for example, Gustavo Gutiérrez, *A Theology of Liberation* (Maryknoll, N.Y.: Orbis, 1973); *The Power of the Poor in History* (Maryknoll, N.Y.: Orbis, 1983).

   The dialectic of negation is very important in the social analysis of Jürgen Habermas. See, for example, Jürgen Habermas, *Theory and Practice* (Boston: Beacon Press, 1973); *Communication and the Evolution of Society* (Boston: Beacon Press, 1979). Habermas has been influential among some Christian social ethicists.
4. For a classic formulation of this doctrine, see Paul Sweazey, *The Theory of Capitalist Development* (New York: Monthly Review Press, 1942). Gutiérrez also makes use of this mode of interpretation.
5. See, for example, Karl Barth, *Community, State, and Church* (Garden City: Doubleday, 1960); *Ethics/Karl Barth*, ed. Dietrick Braun (New York: Seabury Press, 1981); H. Richard Niebuhr, *The Responsible Self* (New York: Harper and Row, 1963).
6. See, for example, Reinhold Niebuhr, *The Nature and Destiny of Man* (New York: Charles Scribner's Sons, 1949); Saul Alinsky, *Reveille for Radicals* (Chicago: University of Chicago Press, 1946).
7. Democratic socialism or democratic capitalism are the preferred modes of political economy among those religious social ethicists willing to express a formal view in favor of one or the other. The study paper moves toward democratic socialism. The Pension Boards Trustees' statement supports democratic capitalism. For a volume incorporating readings of ethicists defending the two modes of political economy, see Bruce Grelle and David A. Krueger, editors, *Christianity and Capitalism* (Chicago: Center for the Scientific Study of Religion, 1986). This volume contains an extensive bibliography on the topic.

8. Marxist modes of thought contrast the current pitiable condition of much of humankind with the greatly enhanced harmony of life with life following the transformation of the political economy. Moltmann appeals to the futurity of God to effect the transformation of humankind. The Wesleyan-Arminian tradition entertains an optimistic view about the power of the person redeemed by God's grace to act in accord with the Divine will. Walter Rauschenbusch and the Social Gospel tradition had substantial hope that the "Christianizing" of the social order would greatly reduce individual selfishness. In his early work, *Moral Man and Immoral Society* (New York: Charles Scribner's Sons, 1932), Reinhold Niebuhr entertained a similar hope. However, in his later work he enlarged his notion of human sinfulness. The redeemed continued to be sinners. For Niebuhr, this reality led him to espouse political democracy and to promote the division of power and the multiplication of factions. See, for example, his *The Nature and Destiny of Man*. Because the study paper has a relatively optimistic view of human nature, divine power, or both, it ignores the propensity of people — including politicians — to pursue their own interests excessively. If the state sought to effect many of the policy proposals advanced in the study paper, its power would be greatly enhanced.
9. See, for example, the work of P. T. Bauer, especially his *Equality, the Third World, and Economic Delusion* (Cambridge: Harvard University Press, 1981), and his *Rhetoric and Reality: Studies in the Economics of Development* (Cambridge: Harvard University Press, 1984). Harry G. Johnson also raises major questions about the efficacy of many of the foreign aid projects. See his *On Economics and Society* (Chicago: University of Chicago Press, 1975). Peter Berger and Michael Novak address problems of Third World development in their *Speaking to the Third World: Essays on Democracy and Development* (Washington, D.C.: American Enterprise Institute for Public Policy Research, 1985). The study paper makes no reference to any of these critics of current foreign aid patterns and practices.
10. Smock, ed., *Christian Faith and Economic Life*, p. 31.
11. Ibid., p. 32.
12. Insofar as economists have been preachers seeking to promote particular values rather than persons seeking to understand the workings of the economic order, they tended to promote growth and efficiency in the nineteenth century and equality in the twentieth century. For a perceptive assessment of these tendencies among economists see George Stigler, *The Economist as Preacher* (Chicago: University of Chicago Press, 1983).

13. The notion of prudential judgments has a long history in Christian social ethics. In his discussion of the four forms of love, Augustine cites prudence as the sagacity to discern what facilitates efforts to promote love and what is a deterrent. In their recent pastoral letter on the U.S. economy, the American Catholic bishops distinguish between their greater certitude about the principles informing their view of economic justice than about their prudential judgments about the best way to embody these principles in the ongoing life of a living community.
14. The text is most dependent on Max Stackhouse's book, *Public Theology and Political Economy* (Grand Rapids: Wm. B. Eerdmans Publishing Co., 1987).
15. *The Market System and American Democratic Polity: Reflections in the Light of Covenantal Tradition*, p. 97. (Page references for this text refer to Appendix page numbers in this volume.)
16. Ibid., p. 102-103. Although the term is not explicitly used in this statement, the paper is offering an ambivalently positive interpretation of American democratic capitalism.
17. Ibid., p. 106.
18. Proposed Pronouncement, "Christian Faith and Economic Life" (undated, distributed by the Secretary of the denomination, April 1989), pp. 10-11.
19. Ibid., p. 13.
20. Proposed Pronouncement, "Christian Faith and Economic Justice" (undated, circulated by the Secretary of the denomination, April 1989), p. 1. The author does not concur with this statement. In his judgment, economic life is the inclusive issue, and economic justice is one of the factors to be considered in deliberations on economic life.
21. Ibid., p. 7.
22. Ibid., p. 9.
23. Ibid., p. 9.
24. Ibid., p. 9.
25. *Proposal for Action*, p. 1.
26. Ibid., p. 1.
27. Proposed Pronouncement, "Christian Faith: Economic Life and Justice" (distributed by the sponsoring bodies, June 1989), p. 1.
28. Proposed Proposal for Action on Christian Faith: Economic Life and Justice, p. 2.

CHAPTER IV

1. *General Synod Handbook, Seventeenth General Synod United Church of Christ, June 29-July 4, 1989* (no cited publisher or date, distributed to Synod delegates in Spring 1989), pp. 16, 18.

2. Ibid., pp. 16, 18.
3. "Sources Used in the Proposed Pronouncement on Christian Faith: Economic Life and Justice," no author cited (June 26, 1989), p. 1.
4. General Synod Seventeen Committee Reports, Part V, "A Pronouncement on Christian Faith: Economic Life and Justice," p. 14. See p. 14 for a listing of the objectives sought.
5. General Synod Seventeen Committee Reports, Part V, "A Proposal for Action on Christian Faith: Economic Life and Justice," p. 23. This proposal originally appeared in a resolution "calling on the United Church of Christ to collaborate with other faith groups in addressing the nation on economic justice," submitted to the General Synod by the Western New York Association of the New York Conference. A staff person in the western area of that conference was a member of the Theology and Economics Covenant Group which developed the study paper and a member of the Pronouncement Committee that drafted the proposed pronouncement, "Christian Faith and Economic Life."
6. Ibid., p. 23.

CHAPTER V

1. In the current epoch, a narrow orthopraxis is a greater danger in the General Synod than a narrow orthodoxy. However, if various forms of liberation theology — emphasizing orthopraxis on principle and sharply blunting, if not obliterating, the distinction between a community of faith and a community of politics — continue to gain popularity among members of ecclesiastical bureaucracies and General Synod participants, at the General Synod level one may see the embodiment of an orthodoxy of orthopraxis. In this author's judgment, such a development would be a matter for grave concern for the churches of the denomination — whatever theological viewpoints they entertain.
2. As best this author can determine, the co-chairs of the original Theology and Economics Covenant Group, M. Douglas Meeks and James Weaver, and the chairperson of the original Pronouncement Committee, Rebecca Blank, were the most influential non-staff persons in the process. As observed previously, Meeks, who contributed very substantially to the study guide, the proposed pronouncement "Chrisitian Faith and Economic Life," and the adopted pronouncement, is very critical of democratic capitalism and promotes policies entailing greater state involvement in the economy. He also shaped the major facets of the document informed by Moltmann's version of "liberation theology" with its

strong emphasis on right conduct. Weaver was a major proponent of the constitutional amendment on economic rights which appeared in the study guide and all three proposed pronouncements. Audrey Chapman, a staff person on the United Church Board for World Ministries, edited the study paper and served on both the Pronouncement Committee and on the committee drafting the proposed version of the adopted pronouncement. She and Blank were major contributors to portions of the study guide and two of the three proposed pronouncements. Both were resource people to the General Synod committee that revised and recommended the "Christian Faith: Economic Life and Justice" document to the General Synod.

The following persons were members of the study group drafting the study paper, the Pronouncement Committee, and the group drafting the final document, "Christian Faith: Economic Life and Justice": Rebecca Blank, Audrey Chapman, Theodore Erickson, and Charles McCollough. Three of these people held staff positions with the national bodies sponsoring the "Christian Faith: Economic Life and Justice" pronouncement.

3. Max L. Stackhouse, Professor of Christian Social Ethics at Andover Newton Theological School, and Roger Shinn, Professor Emeritus at Union Theological Seminary (New York) were both members of the Economics and Theology Covenant Group which produced the study paper. Neither person is an unqualified supporter of American democratic capitalism, but neither one unequivocally espouses a socialist alternative or interprets the American experience in a strongly negative manner.

Professors Stackhouse and Shinn were replaced on the Pronouncement Committee by Walter Brueggemann, Professor of Old Testament, Columbia Theological Seminary, Bonganjalo Goba, who was Associate Professor of Theology and Ethics at the Chicago Theological Seminary at the time the committee was formed, but who became a staff member of the United Church Board of World Ministries before the proposed pronouncement was completed, and Karen Lebacqz, Professor of Christian Ethics, Pacific School of Religion. Douglas Meeks, Professor of Systematic Theology and Philosophy, Eden Theological Seminary, and co-chair of the Economics and Theology Covenant Group, was the other theological seminary professor on the Pronouncement Committee.

This alignment of persons whose theological presuppositions and views on political economy were very compatible, combined with the denominational staff people sharing a strong advocacy viewpoint on the committee, made it almost inevitable that what from other perspectives is a highly sectarian document providing little space for contrasting prudential judgments would emerge from their deliberations.

4. Because the National Conference of Catholic Bishops pastoral letter on the U.S. economy appeals to natural law, it can make such public claims. The warrants the UCC pronouncement advances must be offensive to Jews, Hindus, Buddhists, Shintoists, Muslims, and secularists in our midst. See *Economic Justice for All: Pastoral Letter on Catholic Social Teaching and the U.S. Economy* (Washington, D.C.: National Conference of Catholic Bishops, 1986).
5. It is beyond the scope of this discussion to elaborate this theme. Only a very brief statement is formulated.
6. Section V of the pronouncement, "The Market Economy: Promises and Problems," illustrates this observation very well. Most of the problems cited are in fact persistent, but they have all been addressed in American democratic capitalism. The adequacy of the responses may be questioned, but gross difficulties have been ameliorated.
7. General Synod Committee Reports, Part V, "A Pronouncement on Christian Faith: Economic Life and Justice," p. 9.
8. In this author's judgment, this item should also have noted that the market system encourages people to work diligently and to enhance their skills and competencies. Throughout this pronouncement, human propensities toward lethargy, sloth, and inordinate self-interest are inadequately addressed. It is this author's prudential judgment that these propensities would be increased rather than reduced by a transformation of the American political economy. It is one of the reasons he prefers democratic capitalism to democratic socialism.
9. "A Pronouncement on Christian Faith: Economic Life and Justice," p. 9. This pattern entails a complex interplay of factors, including the age structure of various populations, the racial and ethnic composition of the population, defense spending, the rules and regulations of justice, and contingent historical factors, as well as fiscal and monetary policies.
10. It is interesting that the strengths of a market economy which this author adds all relate to liberty and/or order. Because the pronouncement's drafters did not explicitly cite liberty and order as principles of justice, they may have been insensitive to these cited merits of a market economy.
11. Persons with a very optimistic view of human nature are more willing to give the politicians more power than they already possess.
12. "A Pronouncement on Christian Faith: Economic Life and Justice," p. 9.
13. Ibid., p. 9.

14. Ibid., pp. 9-10. The juxtaposition of these statements is interesting. They probably represent a compromise between the few members of the committee reasonably sympathetic to a market economy and the rest of the drafters.
15. Ibid., p. 10.
16. Ibid.
17. Ibid.
18. Ibid.
19. Ibid., pp. 10-11.
20. Ibid., p. 11. Given the complexity of cultural values required to sustain a market economy, the assertion "market economies especially encourage false values and priorities" needs much more elaboration and clarification. The concern for community values cited here is one of the bases for the perennial appeal of socialism among some people. Greed and materialism existed long before market economies emerged, and they certainly exist in communist societies today.
21. Ibid., p. 11. It is surprising that the impact of multinational corporations was not cited here, for they are the target of substantial critiques in other parts of the pronouncement.

    The unifying effects of the market system in the world are not noted in the pronouncement. Broadly speaking, the burgeoning of the nation-states since 1945 has accentuated the diversity of the peoples of the planet. Without the positive impact of expanding world trade, it is very likely there would have been even more wars and inter-nation conflicts. Institutions in the economic sphere promote regular, continuous and peaceable exchange, in contrast to the irregularity, discontinuity and conflict which acquisition by conquest evokes. It is unfortunate that the pronouncement was not more balanced in the discussion of the expansion of trade and commerce.
22. Ibid., p. 11.
23. In the next section of the pronouncement the call for major institutional changes is repeated. The text reads: "While recognizing the strengths of the market, we must also recognize its limits. We must develop mechanisms within the political system which supplement and reform some aspects of the market economy, rectifying economic injustices and increasing the ability of all individuals to be fully economic participants." Pronouncement, p. 14.

    The drafters of the pronouncement may not be satisfied with the "mechanisms within the political system which supplement and reform some aspects of the market economy," but they should at least acknowledge the substantial mechanisms which have evolved over the past century.

24. For a suggestive discussion of this issue, see Ernest Barker, *Reflections on Government* (London: Oxford University Press, 1967).
25. For an astute analysis of this problem, see Daniel Bell, *The Cultural Contradictions of Capitalism* (New York: Basic Books, 1976).
26. Plato observed long ago that the twin dangers of democracy are mediocrity and anarchy. For a very positive interpretation of the role of elitists in public life, see Hannah Arendt, *The Human Condition* (Garden City, N.Y.: Doubleday, 1958).
27. As cited earlier, in the nineteenth century those relatively few economists who sought to promote their values commended the market economy for its emphasis on growth and efficiency. In the twentieth century, those concerned with expressing their political views have often promoted equality as a desirable social objective.
28. For the views of one who thinks capitalism leads inexorably to uncritical economic growth, see Robert L. Heilbroner, *The Nature and Logic of Capitalism* (New York: W. W. Norton, 1985). For a very sharp critique of liberalism, see Robert P. Wolff, *The Poverty of Liberalism* (Boston: Beacon Press, 1968). For contrasting interpretations, see Julian Simon, *The Ultimate Resource* (Princeton, N.J.: Princeton University Press, 1981). For a critique of persons seeking to limit growth substantially through public policy initiatives, see Edward Walter, *The Immorality of Limiting Growth* (Albany, N.Y.: The State University of New York Press, 1981).

    The extent to which equality and efficiency are contradictory and complementary is debatable. In *Equality and Efficiency: The Big Tradeoff* (Washington, D.C.: The Brookings Institution, 1975), Arthur Okun sees substantial tension between them. On the other hand, Lester C. Thurow in *The Zero-Sum Solution* (New York: Simon and Schuster, 1985) and Robert B. Reich in *The Next American Frontier* (New York: Time Books, 1983) see equality and efficiency as complimentary. Insofar as one attempts to redress inequality by welfare grants not encouraging recipient to work, there is probably tension between equality and efficiency. Insofar as greater equality enhances the quality of the labor force, promotes teamwork between management and labor, and encourages people to make sacrifices to become more efficient, it probably enhances efficiency.
29. "A Pronouncement on Christian Faith: Economic Life and Justice," p. 4.
30. "A Proposal for Action on Christian Faith: Economic Life and Justice", p. 18.
31. General Synod Seventeen Committee Reports, Part V, "A Pronouncement on Christian Faith: Economic Life and Justice," p. 4.
32. Ibid., p. 12.

33. Ibid. One could read these passages dialectically. This author's reading is that some drafters entertained a dialectical reading; others were more optimistic about the consequences of present and future personal and social transformation.
34. The reader is referred to other subsections, particularly that entitled "View of Political Economy," for discussion of related matters. In this subsection, the author addresses more specific policy issues raised in the pronouncement.
35. Economists concerned with economic growth in Africa, Asia, and Latin America have frequently pointed to the need for investment in education. Theodore W. Schultz was a pioneer in this work. See, for example, T. W. Schultz, *Investing in People: The Economics of Population Quality* (Berkeley: University of California Press, 1981).
36. Given the drafters' general orientation, these lacunae are scarcely surprising. In this author's judgment, without greater reliance on the market economy and greater investments in the right kind of education, economic development will continue to languish in many parts of the planet.
37. See, for example, the work of P. T. Bauer and Harry Johnson cited in note 9 of chapter III. See also Peter L. Berger, *The Capitalist Revolution: Fifty Propositions about Prosperity, Equality and Liberty* (New York: Basic Books, 1986).
38. General Synod Seventeen Committee Reports, Part V, "A Pronouncement on Christian Faith: Economic Life and Justice," p. 14.
39. Ibid., p. 2. The rejection of the proposed constitutional amendment will probably have little impact on the actions of the employees of the ecclesiastical bodies which promoted it.
40. From this author's viewpoint, the Biblical Witness Fellowship promotes a narrowly-conceived orthodoxy. The pronouncement errs in the opposite direction, seeking to identify the community of faith with a particular community of politics. Because the pronouncement expresses a viewpoint shared by the majority of General Synod delegates, its narrowness is not as apparent to them as is the narrowness of the Biblical Witness Fellowship. Many people in the denomination are outside the drafters' community of faith as well as outside their community of politics.
41. General Synod Seventeen Committee Reports, Part V, "A Proposal for Action on Christian Faith: Economic Life and Justice," p. 22. The *A Just Peace Church* volume cited is a work produced in response to a pronouncement adopted by a previous General Synod. In addition to the study paper and the pronouncement, the only other denominational document adopted by a national body was the Pension Boards Trustees' statement, *The Market Economy and American Democratic Polity: Reflections in the Light of Covenantal*

Tradition. This document was discussed earlier.

The document promoting the pronouncement largely ignored the Pension Boards Trustees' statement. It was not cited as a resource document in the pronouncement. Pension Boards staff did distribute copies of their statement at the General Synod. Because some speakers at the open hearing on the proposed pronouncement at the General Synod referred to the Pension Boards Trustees' statement, some Synod committee members asked for copies; but its impact on their deliberations was minimal.

In this author's judgment, all the documents promulgated by denominational bodies on the topic are indoctrination pieces, for none of them explores alternative viewpoints with rigor. Nonetheless, because the Pension Boards Trustees' statement reflects a contrasting view to that embodied in the other documents, it would seem to this author that the statement ought to be included among the cited denominational resources in the pronouncement. To its credit, this document did indicate that the Trustees were offering their prudential judgments on these matters and acknowledged the legitimacy of contrasting views within the UCC. Further, it was offered as a statement, not a proposed pronouncement.

42. The Proposal for Action does call on local churches to "support community organizations that enhance the life opportunities and political voice of poor and minority groups, and that increase local economic control" (p. 20). The call does not suggest the ways in which the church is to support community organizations, nor what measures might increase local control. Neither does it explore ways in which local church members could support local community organizations without identifying the church too closely with them.

Appendix

THE MARKET SYSTEM AND AMERICAN DEMOCRATIC POLITY
Reflections in the Light of Covenantal Tradition

A Statement by The Pension Boards United Church of Christ

INTRODUCTION

Formed to express the concern of the United Church of Christ and its predecessor denominations for the retirement needs of its clergy and other employees, The Pension Boards have long been concerned with caring compassion, responsible stewardship and living within the covenant they sustain with members and with the Churches. This spirit of loving care was further intensified with the expansion of services to include health care for the employees of UCC churches and organizations.

When the discussion about "Christian Faith and Economic Life" now in progress within the United Church of Christ, leading to the General Synod in 1989, emerged, it was clear that The Pension Boards should participate. In the 1987-1989 Biennium, the members, churches, Conferences and other organizations of the United Church of Christ are considering the shape of the economic order in the light of their understandings of the Judeo-Christian tradition. Christians differ widely in their prudential judgements about the best means to attain the economic well being of humankind. The Pension Board Trustees here offer their prudential judgements regarding economic life with confidence that this statement will be welcomed by the UCC, its ministers and leaders.

George H. Ellis
Chairman

February 1989

SOURCES OF AUTHORITY

Compassion, stewardship and covenant — clearly central to the Christian Church — are all rooted in the relationship of the living God and the people called by God as seen throughout the Holy Bible. In seeking to be obedient to carry out the commission of God, the Pension Boards have striven to be faithful — as individual Trustees, staff and as an Instrumentality of the United Church of Christ. Since there is such a widespread diversity of ideas regarding the most effective economic arrangement to carry out and demonstrate the Biblical vision, the Pension Boards, along with the other UCC instrumentalities, organizations and churches struggle to identify and maintain the appropriate balance and prioritization among these mandates.

To do this, the Pension Boards have sought to work within sound theological guidelines. There are four ecumenically accepted criteria to which people appeal when they wish to justify the theological and ethical views which they advance, the "quadrilateral sources." The Bible, Tradition, Reason and Personal Experience, or some combination of these sources of authority, are usually used to give legitimacy to the various proposals for theological meaning. Max L. Stackhouse, Herbert Gezork Professor of Christian Social Ethics and Stewardship at Andover Newton Theological School, makes several helpful observations about these criteria.

SCRIPTURE

Everywhere acknowledged as a primary source of authority for Christians, the Bible has had profound significance on Western culture. It is having expanding impact in the Third World, particularly Asia and Africa, as evidenced by the growth of the Church in the nineteenth and twentieth centuries. Stackhouse notes that

> " ... as many other cultures modernize by adopting 'Western' modes of thought as quickly as possible (even while protesting them at every turn), scriptural motifs become contextualized in cultures from which they were not derived."[1]

In the West and in the Third World, there arises the difficulty of understanding the Scriptures outside the context of their origin. Additionally, there is the temptation to select quotations to buttress a particular view of what is true. "We cannot simply repeat what one passage or another says and settle the matter. Nor can we simply pick out the things that we like and leave the rest alone."[2] Yet, Scripture is a primary witness to Jesus Christ and, therefore, central to the Christian faith.

TRADITION

Well described as "the attempt of faith to respond to complex problems not answered explicitly by the events that originally induced the faith and generated the Scriptures,"[3] Tradition does several things. In Tradition we find

> "... not only patterns of worship but also multiple efforts to spell out the criteria (a) for distinguishing between justifiable and unjustifiable uses of coercive power in society, (b) for living with moral integrity in economically and technologically complex civilizations, (c) for the structuring of authority in multiple contexts, and (d) for developing the basic principles of human rights and of viable economic systems. None of these criteria is immediately clear from any of the great scriptures, and to wrestle with these traditions is to recognize the ongoing unveiling of God's purposes in the Tradition that stretches from Biblical days to the modern world."[4]

The caution against reliance upon Scriptures alone for specific criteria to be used in developing basic principles of human rights and viable economic systems should be noted.

REASON

Reason is the process of making judgements by logical thinking which seeks to order information objectively in order to reach a conclusion. Stackhouse observes that many people are skeptical of Reason, yet they use logic, philosophical argument, as well as tests of coherence and consistency to evaluate religious insight.[5]

Reason functions in combination with other sources of authority in formulating prudential judgements.

EXPERIENCE

Human experience contributes to the making of judgements, yet, not all experience is equally important. Stackhouse says:

> "It is difficult to argue that the experience of oppression, injustice, and hate reveals that which we may take as a touchstone of authority. Indeed, it is the experience of creativity, construction, and the overcoming of destruction and decay that is important. ...
>
> The truth and justice that a public theology attempts to articulate is rooted in a God of compassion, and that truth as it is told, as well as we can tell it, must be spoken in love."[6]

THE IMPORTANCE OF COVENANT

The inherent nature of mutual commitment is the underlying basis of services which the Pension Boards render to those who comprise its constituency: clergy, lay-members and churches in the UCC. The notion of Covenant is strong in our denomination. It is a functional relationship between beings, based in Scripture and in the Church. Walter Brueggemann called Covenant, "a way of being committed to each other ... a way of being defined by, accountable to and responsible for each other."[7]

In contemporary usage, covenant applies to defining relationships in what Brueggemann refers to as communities of fate and communities of mutual interest.

The former, communities of fate, normally applies to the families within which we live. The covenant of marriage, e.g., grows into a family covenant, a group of mutual responsibilities and obligations. While our parents chose each other, we did not choose them, nor did we have any voice in their choice of one another! Yet we are all bound together in the structure of our home until the time comes when our own lives lead us into other covenants. While the binding nature of the covenant of fate is perceived to have been weakening in current times, it continues to be a basic community of commitment for most people.

Another covenanted community is the community of mutual interest, or of voluntary association. It is usually a community with limited liability and, whether religious or secular, it seems evident that most people choose such commitments principally with reference to their self-interests. The Rev. Theodore H. Erickson, General Secretary, Division of the American Missionary Association, United Church Board for Homeland Ministries, points out that "... Protestant churches are usually included in this category. While many churches may function as communities of fate rather than communities of mutual interest, in general, American churches survive more by adapting to constituent needs than by proclaiming their historic creeds."[8]

There is yet another dimension of covenant, moreover, in which it can refer to a whole social structure, not just a family or group. Stackhouse observes:

> "Covenant responds to the question of how we humans are to form communities of mutual responsibility as we live out our vocations. People require one another to be whole, and persons in community require a shared framework of common moral obligation that provides the principles by which to structure these relationships.
>
> In the biblical tradition, covenant is seen as a gift of God that bonds the human will to God's justice and to the neighbor in structures of mutual accountability.

> ... Covenant recognizes the need for different levels of accountability in social relationships. It has structures of authority, but it calls leadership to regard, serve and care for those in lower positions. Covenant also recognizes the role of voluntary choice and human agreement ... In short, covenant holds that God set forth terms and limits for our lives together, and that whatever authority we have and however we exercise our wills, we are to be subject to these terms."[9]

The Pension Boards affirm that the United Church of Christ and every one of its Instrumentalities must compassionately seek to carry out the word of Jesus that we are to love one another, even as He loved and was loved by the Creator and Redeemer God. They further acknowledge that, working within the covenant relationship visible throughout the Bible and the tradition of the United Church of Christ, there is mutual responsibility among churches, members and organizations of the Church. This responsibility includes the entire fabric of the social structure. It is in this context, then, that the Trustees believe that their Christian Stewardship is carried out.

THE MANAGEMENT OF CHURCH FUNDS

Along with every board of trustees in UCC Churches, every board of directors and executive committee in UCC organizations and Instrumentalities, and every finance and investment committee in the denomination — be it conference, college, health care institution, every organization through which the UCC ministers to children, the handicapped or retarded or the aging — the Pension Boards grapple with the common question: *How can the resources contributed and invested through tithes, offerings, bequests and members' dues* best *be managed?*

For the entire history of the United Church (since 1957) and long before that in each historic branch of the UCC's predecessor denominations, the standard and accepted methodology has utilized the American banking and market system. The only historical anomaly occurred during the eighteen years from 1934-1952 ... an era which began in the depths of the Great Depression. Tormented with the suffering and difficulty which followed the loss of resources and employment for so many Americans and which threw the plight of the poor into such bold relief, the General Council of the Congregational Christian Churches, by a margin of 130 to 17, condemned the competitive profit-seeking economy and pledged to "work toward the abolition" of that system. They resolved (in 1934) to work toward the abrogation of the market system "by eliminating the system's incentives and habits, the legal forms which sustain it and the moral ideals which justify it."[10] They even set themselves "to modify or eliminate private ownership of the means of production or distribution wherever such ownership interferes with the social good."[11]

After this unhappy eighteen year period, during which the 2nd World War was fought and the Korean War begun, and in response to widely expressed displeasure with the 1934 resolution among many Congregational Christian members, the 1952 General Council disclaimed the 1934 resolution. It is worth noting, however, that there is no record of widespread disposition of equity or bond investments held by the organizations and churches within the denomination during that period in which the market system was held in such low esteem by the church leadership. *Thus*, even at the height of criticism of the market system and the depth of depression and wartime despair, *the practice of the church investment policy continued to rely on the market system as the best available means for multiplying and extending the financial resources of the church to do the Lord's work at home and abroad.*

THE MARKET SYSTEM

During the current reexamination of the rationale, methods and means for the Pension Boards to respond to the constantly changing economy, to relate to the national and world economies and to exercise intelligent Christian stewardship, the Trustees have again appraised the role of the market system and their participation in it.

The Pension Boards' Trustees do not view the market system as free from faults. It is self-evident that there is widespread malaise among many of the partners in the social covenant of public trust which enables the market system to work. *Business abuses of consumer confidence* (fraud in auto-rental insurance charges and fake repairs), *corporate greed* (overcharging by defense contractors), *individual cupidity* (insider trading convictions), *manufacturer irresponsibility* (renewed sales of infant powdered-milk formula in Third World countries), *environmental excesses* (inordinate use of toxic and non-biodegradable materials), *the fouling of America's beaches and rivers* (the criminal ocean dumping of hospital and clinic waste) — ALL cry out for confrontation and corrective countermeasures!

It does not follow, however, that use of the market system as the key arena for the stewardship of church and UCC resources and for the production of goods for the well being of all, should be abandoned; any more than that people should turn against and stop attending church because of the scandals of television evangelists and bilk-the-public money abuses. Indeed, the Trustees of the Pension Boards are convinced that *among the various economic systems available to all nations and investors*, the market system, combined with democratic polity currently in use in the United States, is best able to serve the needs and desires of humanity, including the poor. The market system provides a generally increasing standard of living for the most people while operating with minimum restraint on personal liberty and freedom of choice. The democratic polity facilitates income redistribution, limits gross inequality, and provides for persons of special need. Business abuses must be corrected by both the market and government. *Thus, continued reliance on the market system as a workable means for Christian Stewardship is not only prudent, it is the system most likely to enable the mission of the church.*

ON THEOLOGY AND POLITICAL ECONOMY

The framers of this statement seek additional clarity about the bases underlying the discussion within the UCC of theology and political economy. Advocates of *each* perspective should clearly identify the emphases espoused and the underlying theological, social, political and philosophical basis for their viewpoints. Max Stackhouse is of great assistance to those seeking to understand the appeal and limits of Liberation Theology. He compares differences and similarities of Creationism (Christian fundamentalism) with Liberationism. Noting that they are opposite extremes, Stackhouse says that liberationism focuses on history and its patterns. Its governing question is, "Can humans find fulfillment by social change?"[12]

> "Liberationists answer this question with a clear 'yes,' an answer based on the belief that oppressed peoples are inspired by the Spirit of God to resist the principalities and powers of domination, overthrow the pharaohs of the world, and discover new possibilities of autonomy, freedom, community and human fulfillment. Change — indeed, revolutionary change in history — is the inexorable movement toward the fulfillment of God's divine purpose for humanity.
>
> Liberationism is based on a profound and valid insight that gives it its compelling quality. Liberationists know that the only God worth worshipping is biased in favor of the oppressed, and that truly pious living involves active social engagement for and advocacy of their rights .... They recognize that a compassionate righteousness must be characteristic of every morally and spiritually viable movement in human history. They see that every ideology, regime, program, or plan that pretends to provide salvation for human life is false if it does not challenge the pretense of the arrogant and open horizons of hope to those who suffer. As liberationists rehearse their liturgies of sins — racism, classism, sexism, imperialism, and colonialism — they correctly identify the perils of complex civilizations that arbitrarily arrogate privileges to some and condemn others to positions of fixed inferiority."[13]

The attractiveness of this theological frame-of-reference is compelling for many. Certainly the concerns for justice and the calls to action have roused many clergy and laity from lethargy and indifference into the ranks of the caring and the committed. However, there is less than perfection in liberationism, as Dr. Stackhouse goes on to point out.

> "Frequently, however, these real discernments of evil are wed to a single philosophy of history that is indistinguishable from Marxist dialectics, and that necessitates the consolidation of political, economic, and social power in the hands of a single revolutionary party in the name of the 'people.' Those who share the liberationists' diagnosis of wrong but who offer alternative prescriptions or doubt that radical social change alone can bring human fulfillment are excommunicated, marginalized, silenced or exiled.
>
> The liberationists have seldom made the case for their position much better than the fundamentalists have made the case for their stance. That is why liberationism is often treated as 'ideology' rather than theology ... Liberationists selectively use Scripture in a proof-texting way while criticizing fundamentalists for doing just that."[14]

At this point, Dr. Stackhouse makes an observation regarding the specific use of Old Testament passages which treat the deliverance and redemption of Israel from Egypt from the perspective of liberation theology.

> "For instance, when (the liberationists) select the Exodus as the paradigm of the Bible to govern interpretation, they ignore the Biblical witness about the economic failures in Israel that drove the children into Pharaoh's hands, and they overlook the fact that after the Exodus, the liberated children of Israel preferred the golden calf to the law from the mountain."[15]

One could also observe that the God who ostensibly "entered history" in an "active passion for the poor ... to side with them for justice," fulfilling the Divine "resolve that the slaves should be liberated from the demands of an oppressive system,"[16] permitted every last one of those delivered slaves over twenty years old (and who were among those numbered to go into the Promised Land), to perish in the wilderness because of their faithless murmurings against the God who liberated them and against the leaders empowered by that God to guide them.

Meeting the basic socioeconomic needs of people is always required in the effort to meet the spiritual needs of people. To sever either part of mission from the task distorts the ministry. To emphasize or neglect either the spiritual or socioeconomic needs of those to whom the church would minister seriously weakens the witness and the result of mission.

A market oriented system promotes growth and efficiency in the economic order. This system furnishes an increasing supply of available goods and services of the types people desire, while simultaneously providing the jobs which produce those goods and services. Savings, an essential for an increased standard of living, are marshalled and directed into channels which, in turn, assist in the production of the same goods and services. Decision making and power tend to be dispersed in a market system. Opportunity is provided to generate more income and people have discretionary ability to use that increased income to meet physical, psychological and, in part, spiritual needs. These benefits may come at some social cost, including such problems as job displacement and relocation. Joblessness, poverty and discrimination act to keep many people from directly participating in the market system. For them, the enlarged educational and charitable possibilities produced by that system are critically important as are the corrections of government and the market itself.

Other benefits to society derive from the market system, as well. The value of competition not only provides the public with several choices for the goods or services, but also provides strong incentives to keep prices low. The significance of profits, often misconstrued and misinterpreted, is that they serve primarily as the means for financing the ongoing business operation. Profit is a necessary condition for the system to survive. Without profit, the economic capacity to manufacture goods or provide services would cease.

In addition to fueling the economic engine providing drive to business, another role is played by profits, i.e. the return or reward for investors whose commitment to the venture enabled it to begin operations and create new jobs.

> "In traditional American thinking, the profits of business enterprise have been considered not merely a means for personal pleasure and power, but rather as carrying an obligation to use them for the public good, either through reinvestment in productive facilities or through application to educational or charitable purposes."[17]

The eleemosynary part played by profits generated through the market system in the democratic political environment in the United States cannot be underestimated. The Carnegie Libraries, the medical research of the Sloan-Kettering Foundation, the Ford and Rockefeller Foundation work and the Robert Woods Johnson Foundation contributions to public health ... all have harnessed the profits of market system success which enriched investors beyond their greatest expectations.

Certainly, the returns on investment and the opportunity for growth are key reasons why church organizations have invested major sums over the decades in and through the market system. It is the opinion of the Trustees of the Pension Boards that efforts by the church, particularly the United Church of Christ, to make changes in the social, political and economic order to rectify injustice and meet the needs of the poor and the oppressed, need to be effected without dismantling or undermining the productive economic system in this country, the system which has, directly and indirectly, served so many so well. Following World War II, it also enabled the United States to help rebuild Europe and Japan and, subsequently, to assist many developing nations in the Third World.

The Parables of Jesus recognize that people have differing abilities and resources and that they are accountable to God and other people for the stewardship of those abilities and resources. Trustees of the Pension Boards believe that effective stewardship, enlarged ministry to the poor and oppressed, and increased understanding of economics and the usefulness of the free market system within a democratic political structure are important for UCC members, and are integrally connected aspects of church benevolence. It makes sense to the Pension Boards to favor the economic system which — (despite limits) is *most* likely to facilitate the Gospel imperative to feed the poor and liberate those in captivity.

SUMMARY

The Trustees of the Pension Boards are pleased to offer this statement as a means of participating in the discussion on Christian Faith and Economic Life. The Boards know that there will, in fact, be different judgments made among members and organizations of the UCC about the best means to attain the economic well-being of humankind.

The Pension Boards are very clear in their belief that the historic reliance on the free market system as the means most likely to enable the mission of the church should be continued. Acknowledging that pragmatism plays a real part in such a recommendation, the Boards view the market system in a democratic polity as the best presently available means to meet wisely the challenges of Christian stewardship as we enter the last decade of the 20th Century.

The Pension Boards believe that the advocates of divergent economic philosophies and theologies in the United Church of Christ should listen to each other with respect and learn from each other the key concerns each participant feels. It is critical to maintain unity within diversity, and vice versa.

> "A failure to preserve a diversity of structures and dynamics leads to tyranny. A failure to see how these diversities can and should be ordered coherently leads to anarchy."[18]

The Pension Boards urge UCC church members and Conferences to consider carefully before resolving to support any kind of economic and political transformation. Care needs to be taken to minimize the coalescence of economic and political power. Any system will be imperfect. We must rely on the morality of people operating within the system most likely to achieve our goals. Multiple centers of initiative are desirable to ward-off excessive power in any single center or person.

The Pension Boards also strongly feel that this discussion on economics should be carried out in a spiritual context.

> "God's place in public life is in the middle. God is not elevated above the fray, nor excused from sticky debates. God is with us — Emmanuel. God is a contender. It is the contentious presence of God that frees us from subservience to arbitrary power and calls us to our just responsibilities to each other."[19]

Notes

1. Stackhouse, Max L., *Public Theology and Political Economy*. Grand Rapids: Wm. B. Eerdmans Publishing Co. for the Commission on Stewardship, National Council of the Churches of Christ in the U.S.A., 1987. Page 5.
2. Stackhouse, Max L., Op. cit., Page 7.
3. Op. cit., Page. 9.
4. Loc. cit.
5. Ibid., Page 10.
6. Ibid., Pages 13-14.
7. Brueggemann, Walter, *Address:* "The Risk of Heaven/The Possibility of Faith." General Synod XII, 1979.
8. Erickson, Theodore H., *Address:* "Covenantal Economics." Delivered at A Conference on THE AMERICAN ECONOMY IN TRANSITION at Bethany, West Virginia (Sponsored by the United Church Board for Homeland Ministries) June 1988.
9. Stackhouse, Max L., Op. cit., Pages 26-27.
10. *Digest of Minutes of the Meetings of the General Council of the Congregational Christian Churches of the United States, 1931-1965*. (New York: The Executive Committee of the General Council, 1971) Pages 226-227.
11. Loc. cit.
12. Stackhouse, Max L., Op. cit., Page 21.
13. Loc. cit., Page 22.
14. Ibid., Page 22.
15. Loc. cit.
16. Working Draft: A *Proposed Pronouncement on Christian Faith and Economic Life For the Seventeenth General Synod*, April 1988. Page 2.
17. Worthy, Dr. James C., "Religion and Its Role in the World of Business," *The Chicago Theological Seminary Register*, Vol. XLVIII, No. 3, April 1958. Page 2.
18. Stackhouse, Max L., Op. cit., Page 163.
19. Erickson, Theodore H., Op. cit., Page 6.

Circulated for Discussion and Comments

A PROPOSED PRONOUNCEMENT

CHRISTIAN FAITH AND ECONOMIC JUSTICE

Recommended by the Commission for Racial Justice and the Council for Racial and Ethnic Ministries of the United Church of Christ to the Seventeenth General Synod of the United Church of Christ meeting in Fort Worth, Texas, June 29 - July 4, 1989.

> "A Pronouncement is a statement of Christian conviction on a matter of moral or social principle and has been adopted by a two-thirds vote of a General Synod. It is based on biblical, theological and ethical grounds."

I. SUMMARY

The United Church of Christ vigorously affirms the struggle for economic justice for all of God's peoples as an imperative of our affirmation and understanding of the Christian faith.

II. BACKGROUND

Given the fact that the United Church of Christ faithfully acknowledges its diversity as well as its unity, the racial and ethnic constituencies of the United Church of Christ have been involved in intense dialogue and theological reflection on the issue of Christian faith and economic justice. When the Fourteenth General Synod requested that a representative body of members of the United Church of Christ prepare a pronouncement on the subject of Christian faith and economic life, the racial and ethnic constituency of the United Church of Christ celebrated this opportunity to join in this constructive dialogue. It has long been our collective position that any analysis of the current global economic crisis, or the articulation of a public theology of economics, or the recommending of an appropriate response by the United Church of Christ to the issue of economic life must include the experiences, perspectives and recommendations of the racial and ethnic constituencies of the United Church of Christ.

Representatives of the racial/ethnic special interest groups gathered on July 23, 1988, in Washington, D.C., to provide feedback on the Proposed Pronouncement on Christian Faith and Economic Life. It quickly became apparent that this proposed pronouncement was primarily written through the "lens" or "location" of the majority of the committee members who are white and from the middle and upper strata of this society. Further, it was apparent that this proposed pronouncement did not intend to seriously confront the issue of racism in the context of envisioning appropriate economic life from a Christian faith perspective.

It is our belief that the issue of economic life is an issue of economic justice. We, therefore, believe that the title of the pronouncement to be voted on at the Seventeenth General Synod should more appropriately be named "A Pronouncement on Christian Faith and Economic Justice." Furthermore, this proposed pronouncement reflects a broader perspective, including the concerns of those who primarily do not benefit from the present economic system. The Church cannot be truly prophetic without an honest confession as well as a clear vision. We believe that the Proposed Pronouncement on Christian Faith and Economic Justice offers a clearer and more inclusive vision.

It must be noted, moreover, that the entire Christian church is examining these very issues. For example, as the Roman Catholic church is being impacted by the liberation theology and praxis emerging out of the Third World context, the issues of economic justice and racism are being addressed forthrightly. The National Conference of Catholic Bishops, after much study and deliberation, has released a major 100 page Pastoral Letter entitled "Economic Justice for All: Catholic Social Teaching and the U.S. Economy," which includes a critique of the inequality of the economic system in the United States and throughout the world. In February, 1989, the Pontifical Commission for Peace and Justice at the Vatican issued a major document condemning all forms of racism as sin against the God of justice. The Seventeenth General Synod of the United Church of Christ has an excellent opportunity to make a major statement on the question of economic justice and Christian faith. Mainline Protestant churches in the U.S. must be bold enough to confess the inequity and the injustice of the present economic system in the United States.

The offering of the Proposed Pronouncement on Christian Faith and Economic Justice is an attempt to be faithful participants in the inclusive household of God who demands justice. It is our hope that General Synod Seventeen will rise to the challenge to affirm that the Christian faith demands prophetic action toward economic justice for all God's peoples. In conclusion, the Commission for Racial Justice and the Council for Racial and Ethnic Ministries recommend this pronouncement to the Seventeenth General Synod.

ECONOMIC REALITIES OF THE 1980'S

Economics is a system of connections and interdependence; the word itself comes from the Greek word OIKONOMIA or household. Underlying every economic policy, one can discover the values, morals and philosophy of life upon which it has been based. Martin Luther King depicted the underlying motivating factors behind our present economic system as the forces of **racism, materialism** and **militarism.** (Dr. Martin Luther King, Jr. "A Time to Break Silence", Speech at Riverside Church, April 4, 1967)

Some 32.5 million Americans were living in poverty in 1987 (U.S. Census Bureau). Since 1973, the number of families living in poverty has increased by approximately 2.2 million, an increase of nearly 50 percent. These figures are economic indicators for a period of supposed "economic recovery" and point to the deep economic malaise in which the nation is caught. Furthermore, the middle class, during the past ten years, has been transformed into two-income households. The cost of home ownership and higher education have soared to the point where they are now out of reach. Indeed, we now live in an age where the middle class family can best be characterized as being "a paycheck away from bankruptcy." This has meant homelessness, loss of health insurance coverage, family farm foreclosures, declining quality of life, an environment whose very ability to sustain life is threatened by man made disasters and many other forms of what the Rev. Jesse Jackson termed "economic violence." In addition, a disproportionate share of such hardship has fallen upon racial and ethnic peoples.

A. RACISM

> "The historical record of how white Europeans conquered North America by destroying the native population and how they then built their new nation's economy on the backs of kidnapped Africans who had been turned into chattel are facts that can hardly be denied...White America has yet to recognize the extent of its racism -- that we are and have always been a racist society -- much less to repent of its racial sins." (Jim Wallis, "America's Original Sin: The Legacy of White Racism," Sojourner, 3/22/88)

Racism is the systematized oppression of one race by another. In other words, the various forms of oppression within every sphere of social relations -- economic exploitation, political subordination, cultural devaluation, psychological violation, sexual degradation, verbal abuse, etc. In 1984, the National Council of Churches defined racism as "racial prejudice plus power." This position maintains that privileges conferred upon the white majority by virtue of its racial origins, are supported by a self-sustaining system of institutions and structures which economically benefits from racism. Hence, the Commission for Racial Justice of the United Church of Christ defines racism as "economically-empowered racial prejudice and discrimination." (Civil Rights Journal -- Commentary #359)

In specific terms, these policies translate into an unemployment rate in American Indian communities ranging from 70% to 90%. Alcoholism, and other forms of substance abuse, has touched about 90% of individuals in the American Indian community. The spiritual devastation that resulted from the multi-dimensioned experience of cultural genocide has also led to a high suicide rate among our American Indian sisters and brothers.

Likewise, economic motivations played a hidden role in the internment of Japanese-Americans during World War II, using war hysteria as a smokescreen for the stealing of land and other possessions. The majority of Japanese Americans in Hawaii were not put in concentration camps like their counterparts in California and other western states because most of them were lowly-paid pineapple and sugar plantation workers in 1942. Japanese Americans, however, owned land in California and were supplying approximately 90% of the vegetable crop in the state.

The General Synod 16 Pronouncement on "The Hispanic Ministry of the United Church of Christ" documents the impoverishment taking place within Hispanic communities. Hispanics, 85% of whom live in urban areas, is a disproportionately poor group living in substandard inner-city housing. In 1986, the unemployment rate among Hispanics (persons of Spanish Origin) was 10.6%. The poverty rate for Hispanics was 28.2% in 1987, significantly higher than the already elevated rate of 21.9% in 1977. Robert Greenstein of the Center on Budget and Policy Priorities, in his speech to the National Consultation on Children in Poverty (February, 1988), indicated that over the last eight to ten years, poverty spread more rapidly among Hispanics than among any other group. Even with the historical Census undercount of Hispanics, the percentage of Hispanics without health insurance coverage is a phenomenal 27.0%.

African Americans, who were forcibly brought to the U.S. as slaves, continue to suffer from economic exploitation. Today, whites enjoy 12 times the net worth of African-Americans. The median net worth of African-American households is $3,400, compared to $39,100 for white households. These figures reflect not only the lower value of African American owned property, such as housing, but an unemployment rate of 14.5% in 1986 compared to a white unemployment rate of 6.0%. African Americans between ages 16-19 suffered a staggering rate of 39.3%. This cycle of continuing poverty is underscored by a recent report of the New York State Task Force on the Education of Children and Youth At Risk, which concluded that New York has two separate but unequal public school systems: one in the areas where the predominantly white rich live and the other in the areas where the predominantly African American and Hispanic American poor live.

B. MATERIALISM

> "Those who believe in capitalism must fight back... We practice good business and good citizenship in every country. As a result, we are welcomed by the people and governments, wherever we are involved." (The late D.J. Kirchhof, former president of Castle and Cooke Inc. (Dole) in Barron's National Business and Financial Weekly, Feb. 19, 1979.)

During the period 1969 to 1980, Americans learned some new terms such as "capital flight", "economic dislocation," and "plant closures." During this period, almost everything unionized that could be moved to a nonunion state or country was moved. Because manufacturing was the most heavily unionized sectors of the U.S. economy capable of moving, they were the first to move. Corporations engaged in active union busting combined with the conscious support for regimes and political powers that repressed union organizing.

For example, Castle and Cooke (Dole) moved pineapple production from Hawaii to the Philippines in response to the farmworkers' effective organizing efforts in Hawaii. An interesting note is that Samuel Castle and Amos Cooke were former Congregationalist missionaries to Hawaii, who turned their missionary zeal to entrepreneurial efforts in 1852. Andrew Cortez, a lay leader in the Philippine Independent Church, was a labor organizer. In 1983, as a result of his organizing work, Andrew was abducted by the Philippine military. Andrew's captors cut slits all over his body. At night they stitched the cuts with coarse thread and a rusty needle. The next day, they ripped open the stitches and in the evening they sewed Andrew's cuts again. This procedure continued until he died of his infected, open wounds. What the military did to Andrew Cortez was clearly designed for its chilling effect on other organizers. (Dorothy Friesen, Critical Choices, 1988).

Similarly, the U.S. farmer is being displaced by agribusiness. The accompanying problems of pesticides and toxic poisoning and exploitation of farmworkers continue their upward spiral. In addition, a service economy has replaced the manufacturing sector which moved overseas. The service economy includes huge corporations which provide janitorial, secretarial and security services. The biggest trend is towards a contingent workforce which means one is a casual, on-call, involuntary part-time or self-employed worker with no benefits. A full 25% of the workforce now falls into this category; the Temporary Help Supply (THS) industry is growing seven times faster than all other non-agricultural industries. (Employment Development Department (EDD), January 1988).

One result of this new corporate service economy has been a loss of real income and dignity for American families, not to speak of those groups who consistently have little or no income at all. Since reaching a peak in 1973, real U.S. wages declined by 15 percent. (Dollars and Sense, January-February, 1989) The congressional Joint Economic Committee reports that 60% of all jobs created since 1979 pay less than $7,000 a year. Thus, government statistics are misleading, causing one to one incorrectly assume that Americans have benefited by greater employment. However, many families made up part of this loss by sending the mother/wife to work at great sacrifice to the quality of life. Even worse has been the situation of female-headed households with children and households headed by persons with disabilities. Nearly 2/3 of persons with disabilities are not in the workforce due to work disincentives.

The lower standard of living is not shared by all. In 1986, Chief Executive Officers (CEO's) of Fortune 500 companies averaged $931,800. An average worker earned $19,750. During the past eight years, the rich have won and the average worker has lost. We have now reached an incredible state where the top 2% of U.S. families own 30% of liquid assets, 50% of corporate stock owned by individuals, 39% of all corporate and government bonds, 71% of tax exempt municipal bonds and 20% of all real estate. (William Greider, "Secrets of the Temple," New Yorker magazine, 11/9/87)

Essentially the last two decades, and the 80s in particular, have been characterized by a massive redistribution of wealth. This upward shift to a small group created by globalization, deregulation and privatization has been based on the belief that competition brings out the best in persons and on the myth that all persons are competing equally.

C. MILITARISM

> "When I give food to the poor they call me a saint; when I ask why the poor have no food, they call me a communist." (Dom Helder Camara, Archbishop of Recife, Brazil)

Martin Luther King, Jr., in his Riverside Church speech in April 1967 said, "A deeper malady afflicts the American spirit, of which Vietnam is but a symptom." This deeper sickness has to do with the Cold War and the pathological anti-communism that has become institutionalized in the thinking of most Americans. The Cold War has been used to justify the spending of $300 billion a year on weapons of mass destruction while 3 million homeless persons sleep on the streets and 460,000 farmers in this decade lose their farms because they could not get a loan from the government to hold them over until spring planting.

The centerpiece of the Cold War is the escalation of militarism; it is not a search for political solutions to the differences between the Soviet Union and the U.S. Furthermore, anti-communist ideology is a useful tool to suppress legitimate demands by persons who are victimized and at the bottom of the market system, both in the United States and abroad. Poor farmers fighting for land reform in Third World countries are quickly labeled "communists", as are justice and peace workers in the U.S. who ask the question, "Why are people hungry?" What would Jesus be labeled today for his work with the poor and outcast in society?

The U.S. government today is aligned with people and governments all over the world who want to keep power and wealth in the hands of the few. This policy is necessary to protect U.S. transnational global interests in the areas of market, raw materials and cheap labor. Unfortunately for the people of the world, the Cold War has been a very effective tool of the U.S. military/industrial complex in obtaining billions of dollars from U.S. taxpayers to fight against the birthing of a just economic order in the world.

The debt crisis was not produced by a chance concatenation of events. As one top Bank of America executive admitted, "the greed of bankers" was central to the process which engendered the international debt crisis. ("International Debt and Economic Justice for All", Conference, Santa Clara, Ca., May 6, 1987) Lending by New York banks was concentrated in a few countries. In addition to Mexico, the preferred customers were Brazil, Argentina, Chile, South Korea and the Philippines. A common characteristic of these countries throughout the seventies and early eighties was that they were ruled by military-technocratic elites. The surface "stability" of an authoritarian order, in other words, provided the bankers with the reassurance that their loans would be repaid.

> "Authoritarian governments appealed to the bank manager who, after all, came from an institution with basically authoritarian structures... It was so attractive--people like Delfim Netto (of Brazil) came across as standing for unifying the country, politics, and stability. They were good CEOs." (Walden Bello and Claudio Saunt, S.F., June 1987 interview)

The debt crisis did not stem from Third World countries living beyond their means, as conventional wisdom would have it. The International Monetary Fund (IMF) and the World Bank, the two Western-controlled agencies that monitor international capital flow, had a role in creating this crisis. In their Third World lending, the private banks depended a lot on the IMF's and World Bank's estimates of a country's worthiness. Contrary to its image of being an impartial watchdog over Third World finances, the IMF made exceptions based on ideological considerations. Invariably, evidence of massive capital flight, waste, and mismanagement was systematically overlooked by the Fund and the Bank.

Considerable space has been devoted to elucidating the prime cause of the debt crisis in order to build a case that repudiation of the debt is a just course of action. Economic justice for the millions of persons in numerous Third World nations who not only have had no part in the decisions of bankers and dictators that led to this massive indebtedness demands going beyond "debt forgiveness" to a genuine repentance on the part of those who control the world economic order, i.e., the International Monetary Fund and the World Bank. In other words, the Christian faith envisions a "beloved community" globally where the financial and natural resources of the world are equitably shared and consumed.

III. BIBLICAL, THEOLOGICAL AND ETHICAL RATIONALE

The Christian faith commends the life, ministry and teachings of Jesus Christ as instruction for Christian social action. The God of justice, as self-disclosed in the life, death and resurrection of Jesus Christ, demands that the community of faith, the Christian church, remain active participants in the inclusive household of God. The God of justice is also the God of creation and the God of salvation.

One of the basic tenants of the Christian faith is that the living God, through God's inestimable grace and love for humankind, exists in each and every one of us and that we are each called to love and serve that same God, and we are called to love and do justice for all of God's peoples. The Bible begins with the story of God's creation.

> "So God created man in his own image, in the image of God he created him; mal and female he created them. And God blessed them, and God said to them, 'Be fruitful and multiply, and fill the earth and subdue it; and have dominion over the fish of the sea and over the birds of the air and over every living thing that moves upon the earth.'" (Genesis 1: 27-28)

Thus, we affirm that God created all human beings equally in the image of God, imago Dei. The Statement of Faith of the United Church of Christ affirms:

> "We believe in God, the Eternal Spirit, who is made known to us
> in Jesus our brother and to whose deeds we testify:
> God calls the worlds into being, creates humankind in the divine image,
> and sets before us the ways of life and death.
> God seeks in holy love to save all people from aimlessness and sin.
> God judges all humanity and all nations by that will of righteousness
> declared through prophets and apostles."

Fundamentally, the capitalist economic system profits from the exploitation, manipulation and monopolization of human as well as financial resources. Inherent in the capitalist economic system is the notion that material profit and the accumulation of capital is more important than an equitable sharing of the wealth of society. This notion contradicts the basic tenants of love and justice as affirmed by the Christian faith. Economic justice in the United States from a Christian perspective would require a transformation of the capitalist economic system.

> "The Spirit of the Lord is upon me, because God has anointed me to preach good news to the poor. God has sent me to proclaim release to the captives and recovering of sight to the blind, to set at liberty those who are oppressed, to proclaim the acceptable year of the Lord."
> (Luke 4:18)

These are the imperatives with which Jesus chose to begin his public ministry. These Gospel imperatives should must stay in the forefront of the Christian ministry today.

Indeed, the entire Old Testament is also filled with prophetic stories of God caring for the needs of God's human family, especially those who are seeking justice. Perhaps the most striking story of God's justice for the oppressed is that of the exodus and God's freeing of God's people from generations of economic bondage. The covenant that God made with the people of Israel shows a special concern for those most vulnerable. (Ex.20:22-23:33) Moreover, God demands justice for all and executes justice for the poor. (Ps 140:12)

In addition to proclaiming the word of God, Jesus lived the word of God. Through his every action, he resisted temptations of wealth and power, of seeking an earthly kingdom. He healed the sick, he ate with outcasts and walked with sinners. Jesus identified with the powerless who yearned and struggled to be liberated from the sins of oppression.

It was for each of us that Jesus died and through his death, the new covenant with God is begun. Thus, our baptism as Christians signifies our new life with Christ and calls us to be faithful witnesses of the work of Jesus Christ. It calls us to take the side of those who are poor, those who are suffering, those who are most in need. As Christians, we can do no less.

> "When you lift your hands in prayer, I will not look at you. No matter how much you pray, I will not listen, for your hands are covered in blood. Wash yourselves clean. Stop all this evil and learn to do right. See that justice is done--help those who are oppressed, give orphans their rights, and defend widows." (Isaiah 1:15-17)

God's word to us through Isaiah is indeed a challenge to all churchgoers in the United States. The hands of most U.S. citizens who pay taxes to the government are bloody since 40 to 60 percent of the national budget goes to war costs. In Critical Choices, (1988), Dorothy Friesen, a Mennonite, writes:

> "As residents in this imperial nation, we face not only economic and military entanglement. We are also subject to the spiritual desolation that results from our collective pathology... "

God's judgment upon a nation and its people inebriated by privilege and comfort at the expense of the many can be seen in the meaningless of life experienced by so many in our culture. The drug culture, the high suicide rates among teenagers, the fearful society are all symptoms of a deep malady. The illness can only be cured by actively living the Gospel of Jesus Christ which necessitates the cleaning of our bloodied hands and being committed to struggle for economic justice.

In the New Testament we are reminded that our calling as disciples of Christ is to servanthood, not to a life of privilege and status. True servanthood leads to new challenges, struggle, and victories for Christ, which will lead to new life and a new creation, i.e., a new global economic order of justice.

IV. STATEMENT OF CHRISTIAN CONFESSION/CONVICTION

The UCC Statement of Mission reads: "Empowered by the Holy Spirit, we are called and commit ourselves... to praise God, confess our sin, and joyfully accept God's forgiveness..."

In that spirit, the members of the United Church of Christ, its instrumentalities, local churches, associations, conferences, and all national bodies confess that we live in a privileged society which has committed economic injustices in the world. We are called to confess that from places of privilege it is difficult to stand in solidarity with the poor and the oppressed.

We are called to confess that our statements of concern for the poor do little to finally correct the economic injustices in the world.

We are called to "name and confront the powers of evil within and among us." That evil is the worship of mammon in all its forms, to which we have fallen prey.

We are called to "repent our silence and complicity with the forces of chaos and death."

Furthermore, we are called to live out the commandment of Jesus: "You shall love the Lord your God with all your heart, and with all you soul, and with all your mind, and with all your strength... you shall love your neighbor as yourself (Mark 12:29-31)"
As we confess and repent, we declare our intention to work and struggle for a nation in which every human being lives fully in dignity, empowerment and joy. We declare our intention to work for the passage of a constitutional amendment calling for an economic bill of rights that will provide:

-- A guaranteed national minimum income level, below which no person or family should be allowed to live, ensuring every person access to food, clothing and shelter;
-- A national health program available to all persons;
-- A quality education system that provides to every person nurture, enrichment and education from infancy to adulthood;
-- A governmentally guaranteed right to employment consistent with each person's potential;
-- A guaranteed right of every person to permanent, affordable, quality housing.

As we confess and repent, we also declare our intention to work for a world in which every human being lives fully in dignity, empowerment and joy. As an act of Christian faith, we declare our intention to struggle against U.S. interventions in other countries which attempt to dominate the economic, political and social well-being of the citizens of those countries. We move to struggle against the misuse of U.S. military and economic aid in U.S. neo-colonies in Asia, Central America, Africa and the Middle East. True national security for all means the elimination of covert and overt operations which attempt to maintain an unjust global economic system where only five percent of the world's population utilizes 40 percent of the world's resources.

As we confess and repent, we declare our intention to refrain the easy use of labels such as "left-wing", "Communist" and "Marxist" to dismiss the uncomfortable realities of global economic injustice. As a church we must move from merely doing acts of charity to asking the questions, "Why?... Why are people poor?" and "What does the Christian faith demand that we do to ensure economic justice for all of God's peoples?"

Circulated for Discussion and Comment

PROPOSAL FOR ACTION

CHRISTIAN FAITH AND ECONOMIC JUSTICE

Recommended by the Commission for Racial Justice and the Council for Racial and Ethnic Ministries of the United Church of Christ to the Seventeenth General Synod of the United Church of Christ meeting in Fort Worth, Texas, June 29 - July 4, 1989.

> "A Proposal for Action is a recommendation for specific directional statements and goals implementing a Pronouncement."

I. SUMMARY

This Proposal for Action delineates the strategies by which all parts of the United Church of Christ should work for economic justice as an imperative of our affirmation and understanding of the Christian faith.

II. BACKGROUND STATEMENT

This Proposal for Action is based upon the Pronouncement on Christian Faith and Economic Justice. The Pronouncement presents a policy statement for the United Church of Christ on the issue of economic justice. This Proposal for Action, therefore, delineates a specific program of action strategies that will enable the United Church of Christ to become effectively involved at all levels in the struggle to ensure that economic justice is a reality for all of God's peoples in the United States and throughout the world.

This Proposal for Action further seeks to implement, through Christian social action, the programmatic thrust of the Pronouncement on Christian Faith and Economic Justice which seeks to remain faithful to the Statement of Faith and the Statement of Mission of the United Church of Christ.

III. DIRECTIONAL STATEMENT AND GOALS

As people of the United Church of Christ, affirming our Statements of Faith and Mission, we seek within the Church Universal to participate in God's mission of economic justice for all of God's peoples and to follow the way of liberation of the crucified and risen Christ . . .

We have confessed and stated our Christian conviction to struggle against all forms of economic injustice in this nation and throughout the world ...

We firmly establish as a goal the just transformation of the capitalist economic system into an economic system that fundamentally ensures economic, racial and social justice and equality in the United States ...

We further firmly establish as a goal the just transformation of the global economic order into an economic order that fundamentally ensures economic, racial and social justice for all of God's peoples throughout the world ...

Based on this confession and affirmation, the Seventeenth General Synod calls for the adoption of the following actions.

IV. CALL TO MEMBERS, LOCAL CHURCHES, ASSOCIATIONS, CONFERENCES, INSTRUMENTALITIES AND OTHER NATIONAL BODIES, SEMINARIES AND OTHER RELATED INSTITUTIONS OF THE UNITED CHURCH OF CHRIST

The Seventeenth General Synod calls upon all members of the United Church of Christ to actively work at the local level to challenge all forms of economic injustice by engaging in:

1. Prayer and theological reflection on the basic tenets of the Christian faith in order to more clearly understand the imperatives of God's mission of economic justice.

2. Denominational and ecumenical public worship which consistently motivates Christian social action toward the goal of economic justice for all of God's peoples.

3. Personal and corporate economic evaluations on how to more faithfully contribute personal and corporate financial resources to the cause of economic and racial justice and equality in this nation and throughout the world.

4. Study and action groups that are designed to facilitate personal and corporate involvement in the transformation of the present economic system in this nation and throughout the world.

The Seventeenth General Synod calls upon all local churches of the United Church of Christ to respond affirmatively to God's demand for economic justice for all of God's peoples by:

1. Proclaiming the liberating Gospel of Jesus Christ in public worship which exemplifies the justice-seeking ministry of Christ in the world in which we live.

2. Encouraging all members and all those who worship in the church to be actively engaged in prayer, reflection and effective social action toward the goal of economic justice.

3. Implementing a program of Christian education that informs and challenges all participants to know and to confess the sins of the present economic system and to make a commitment for involvement in developing a more just economic system.

The Seventeenth General Synod calls upon all Associations and Conferences of the United Church of Christ to adopt economic justice policies, priorities and programs that will lead to:

1. Establishment of committees for economic justice at the association and conference levels.

2. Research and development of a critical analysis of the injustice of the present economic system and to present recommendations on how associations and conferences can be more faithful participants in the transformation of the present system into a system of economic justice.

The Seventeenth General Synod calls upon all Instrumentalities and other National bodies and Seminaries and other related institutions of the United Church of Christ to affirmatively and programmatically respond to the call for economic transformation of the present economic system and to work diligently for economic justice by:

1. Establishing and developing national and regional programs and projects which are centered on the goal of economic justice in the United States and throughout the world.

2. Researching and publishing critical and constructive analyses of the present economic system and to make recommendations that ensure the attainment of a just transformation of the present economic system in the interest of economic justice.

3. Continuing to promote and advocate divestment from all corporations doing business in South Africa and other nations where economic and racial oppression are commonplace.

4. Developing new and more effective programmatic relationships with sisters and brothers in the Third World which enhance the global struggle toward economic justice.

5. Providing national and international leadership toward the development of an effective global ecumenical movement for economic justice which has as its central goal the just transformation of the global economic order.

V. IMPLEMENTATION

The Seventeenth General Synod requests the Commission for Racial Justice, the Office for Church in Society, the United Church Board for Homeland Ministries, the United Church Board for World Ministries, the Office of Communication and the Office Life and Leadership to jointly coordinate the implementation of this Proposal for Action, with monitoring by the Council for Racial and Ethnic Ministries, and requests that a detailed report be made to the Eighteenth and succeeding General Synods.

A PRONOUNCEMENT ON CHRISTIAN FAITH: ECONOMIC LIFE AND JUSTICE

"A Pronouncement is a statement of Christian conviction on a matter of moral or social principle and has been adopted by a two-thirds vote of a General Synod. It is based on biblical, theological and ethical grounds."

I. SUMMARY

This pronouncement is an affirmation by the United Church of Christ that the struggle to achieve economic justice for all of God's people is an imperative of the Christian faith. It is also a confession that we have done too little to correct the economic injustices of our nation and the world. Finally, it is a statement of our commitment to transform the structures of church and society by working for economic justice.

II. BACKGROUND

There is a sickness in the soul that infects both the poor and the affluent in our nation and the world as a result of economic injustice. Among the poor are those who have internalized economic powerlessness and poverty, losing a sense of meaning and worth to their lives. Among the affluent are those who have been captured by the false values and priorities of materialism and who have also lost a sense of the meaning and purpose of life. An unjust economy generates dissatisfaction for both those with too much and those with too little.

For Christians, economic justice is a faith issue, "for the Lord is a God of justice" (Is. 30:18). Scripture discloses a God whose love and compassion for creation have no limits, a God "who executes justice for the oppressed; who gives food to the hungry" (Ps. 146:7), a God who in Jesus Christ came "that they may have life, and have it abundantly" (Jn. 10:10). Moreover, there is pervasive poverty and suffering in the midst of those economic systems which are capable of organizing the gifts of creation so that all members of the human household could have the means of life. In such a situation, commitment to economic justice becomes a profound human responsibility. In the parable of the great judgement, Jesus reminds individuals and nations that in failing to provide food to the hungry, drink to the thirsty, welcome to the stranger, clothing to the naked, and care to the infirmed and imprisoned "as you did it not to one of the least of these, you did it not to me" (Mt. 25:45).

This pronouncement attempts to portray the experiences and perspectives of both those victimized by present economic systems as well as those who benefit from those systems. It is motivated by the cries of anguish of our sisters and brothers in our nation and the world. Remembering God's special concern for the poor and suffering, the pronouncement seeks to understand why current economic systems fail to provide an adequate means of life for two-thirds of the members of the human community.

The Pronouncement on Christian Faith: Economic Life and Justice builds on the Pronouncement Affirming the United Church of Christ as a Just Peace Church voted by the Fifteenth General Synod. It presents the call to economic justice as a complement to the focus on peace in that earlier pronouncement.

The pronouncement is the outgrowth of a long process of study and reflection. In 1980, a group of United Church of Christ theologians and economists made a covenant together "to join the search for new economic theories and strategies more faithful to the Gospel." The Fourteenth General Synod requested the preparation of a pronouncement containing an analysis of the global economic crisis from a Christian perspective, an articulation of a public theology of economics, and an appropriate response by the United Church of Christ.

This pronouncement is the synthesis of two documents: the Proposed Pronouncement on Christian Faith and Economic Life and the Proposed Pronouncement on Christian Faith and Economic Justice, both of which have been submitted to the Seventeenth General Synod. The proposed Pronouncement on Christian Faith and Economic Life was informed by feedback to the study paper, Christian Faith and Economic Life, provided by a diverse group of United Church of Christ members. The racial and ethnic members of the United Church of Christ believed that the relationship between racism and economic injustice needed further articulation; this was provided in the Proposed Pronouncement on Christian Faith and Economic Justice.

This pronouncement recognizes that the majority of people in the world suffer in one way or another under the present global economic order, irrespective of their particular economic system. As North American Christians in the United Church of Christ, we must boldly confess the inequity and injustice in the economic system of the United States, at the same time that we admit our involvement with injustices in the global economy. This confession requires both naming the structural problems inherent in our economic system and confronting the effects of racism, sexism, materialism and militarism. The church cannot be truly prophetic without honest confession.

As we struggle to understand the demands of justice that God places on our economic lives, we acknowledge that we, in the United Church of Christ, come from many different economic backgrounds. Our personal histories affect how we hear the Word, particularly when economic issues are at stake. Thus, rich and poor in our church respond very differently to the news that the hungry were fed and the rich sent away empty (Lk. 1:53). Some who are poor among us hear this word and cry out for immediate change. Some who are affluent among us let the fear of loss keep us from fully hearing the judging and transforming message. Those who are comfortable often focus on the benefits of the current economic system and hope that charity and economic growth will ameliorate suffering and poverty. But those whose children go to bed hungry at night, those who have no home or means of income cannot wait.

This pronouncement is being offered by the United Church Board for World Ministries, the United Church Board for Homeland Ministries, the Commission for Racial Justice, the Office for Church in Society, and the Council for Racial and Ethnic Ministries.

III. BIBLICAL, ETHICAL AND THEOLOGICAL RATIONALE

The word "economy" comes from two Greek words meaning "household," and "law" or "management." (The compounded Greek word is often translated "stewardship.") Economy therefore is the ordering or management of the household. For Christians, economics involves the management of the human household in a manner consistent with God's intentions as revealed in scripture. Many of the biblical traditions depict God's desire for a just household in which all persons, particularly the poor and vulnerable, have access to resources sufficient for survival, freedom, dignity and community participation.

The formative event of biblical faith is the Exodus, God's liberation of slaves from the oppressive household or economy of Pharaoh. God disrupts the productive but deadly economy of Pharaoh because some of its slaves cry out to God under their burdens. After delivering the people of Israel, God establishes a covenanted household of justice in the land of promise. The first five books of the Old Testament describe a three-way covenant linking God, the human family and the whole earth, balancing the needs of humanity and of nature (Lev. 25:1-7, 11-12). The covenant makes clear that economic activity should be ordered to reflect the mutual obligations between God and the human community. Israel's economy should be grounded in God's justice.

Repeatedly, the covenant of the Old Testament focuses on the needs and rights of those who often are excluded from the community. The rules of God's household demand that the poor (Ex. 23:6, Deut. 15:7-11), the stranger (Ex. 22:21-24), the sojourner (Deut. 10:19), and the widow and orphan (Ex. 22:22) all be accorded special protection and access to the livelihood of the household for the sake of God's grace to Israel ("for you were strangers in the land of Egypt" Ex. 22:21). The Sabbath and Jubilee Year urge a just ordering for overcoming exploitation through property redistribution and care of the earth. God's household is ordered to protect its weakest and most vulnerable members (Lev. 25:8-22). The same God who brings the universe into being and provides the earth with abundance intends that the needs of all God's creatures be met (Gen. 1:27-31). God's justice (Ps. 99:4) is opposed to patterns of economic inequality and power that leave some marginalized and others dispossessed.

When Israel establishes an empire with a king, the poor, the weak, and the oppressed become central to God's economic concern. In the household of Israel, the king was called to have concern for the weak, save the lives of the poor, and liberate them from oppression and violence (Ps. 72:12-14, cf. Jer. 22:15-16). When their ordering of Israel's household generates affluence but exploits or ignores the poor, God's prophets challenge Israel's kings to account. Prophetic denunciation of such royal economic policy is pervasive in the Old Testament, and prophetic judgment includes the warning that God will disrupt the order of Israel's household for the sake of the poor even as God has disrupted Pharaoh's household (Isa. 10:1-3, Amos 4:1-2, Jer. 22:13-14).

In Jesus, God becomes poor (II Cor. 8:9) and shares the suffering, the life, and the death of the poor and dispossessed. God in Jesus Christ reigns as no other ruler, not set above, but in suffering love with all people. It is this God who is God in every dimension of our life -- spiritual and economic, secular and sacred (Ps. 24:1, Col. 1:15-21). According to the Gospel of Luke, Jesus inaugurates his public ministry by announcing that he has been anointed to preach good news to the poor, to proclaim liberty to the captives, and to set at liberty the oppressed (Lk. 4:18). Jesus' public ministry is the announcement that God's household is open to all to whom it had been systematically closed by rules of the world's economy.

The world of Jesus is the world of Rome, a most efficient, successful and yet corrupt political economy. The empire's economy, for those who were able and willing to compete successfully within its household rules, was at its peak. Yet the focus of Jesus' life and ministry was not these people. In his preaching we encounter again and again a challenge to economic greed and oppression that is based on the values of accumulation and exploitation. In the sayings and actions of Jesus the reign of God's justice reverses precisely those values upon which the human economy depends for its success:

> Blessed are you poor ...
>   Woe to you who are rich...
> Blessed are you who hunger...
>   Woe to you who are full...
> Blessed are you who weep...
>   Woe to you who laugh ...
> Blessed are you when people despise you and exclude you...
>   Woe to you when people speak well of you... (Lk. 6:20-26)

Through his own table fellowship among the excluded, his signs and wonders among the outcasts, and in his crucifixion outside the gates, Jesus took on himself the suffering of God with the poor and all who are excluded from justice within the household. Through Jesus' resurrection God proclaims that abundant life is for all. In Christ, the covenant of love and justice in the household is made new and is expanded to the whole human family. The early church, in faithfulness to Jesus' life, death, and resurrection, held in tension the coming reign of God and the values which undergird the human economy. In ordering its household the early church rejected many of the principles operative within the larger economy. In its expectation of God's reign, it embraced both the life of the community as the basic motivation for economic production and human need as the basic principle of distribution within the household of God (Acts 2:44-45). It sought to follow Jesus' own orientation to those marginalized by the injustice of the political economy (James 5:4-6).

The reign of God coming in our midst is a continual invitation to repentance, for all economic systems fall short of reflecting the household of God and the covenant is continually breached by injustice. As Christians we must acknowledge that we cannot witness to the reign of God and also serve mammon (Mt. 6:24). Our economic lives are as subject to God's grace and God's judgment as our spiritual lives. We shrink from this acknowledgment, however, because we are afraid to bear the suffering love of Christ in our own lives. We resist because we find our own vested interests challenged if we are faithful to God's covenant. We hesitate, for to acknowledge the reign of God and justice is to expose our loyalty to mammon and we are unmasked as idolaters. Yet it is promised that through faith, hope, and love God can bring our lives into repentance. We are both haunted and energized by the certainty that God will continue to judge us, transform us, and empower us until the rule of justice prevails in the human household.

Through our baptism into the body of Christ we are commissioned to participate with God in the just reordering of our economy. We stand under the demand of God that the economy be reorganized so that the poor may also share in the abundance of creation and be poor no more (Deut. 15:4-5). As stewards of the household, we are called to care for creation so that all members of the household will have "their portion of food at the proper time" (Lk. 12:42).

IV. SUFFERING WITHIN THE HOUSEHOLD OF GOD

A. POVERTY AND AFFLUENCE

> I am a citizen of the United States and a child of God, and so are my children. We are not just statistics. We are real human beings. (Cheryl Kramer, mother of four from Iowa)

Cheryl Kramer was forced by her economic situation to give up her children to foster care. Theirs is the human anguish behind the statistic that families with children are the "fastest growing" segment of the homeless, according to a recent National Academy of Sciences study. There are over 100,000 children homeless each night, with perhaps a quarter million children who experienced homelessness at some time during 1988.

Within the United States, one of the wealthiest countries in the world, economic growth and affluence have not eliminated significant levels of poverty. In 1987, 8.2 percent of white families lived below the poverty level. With respect to white families and African American families with a female head of household, 26.7 percent and 51.8 percent lived below the poverty level respectively. One fifth of all children in this country live in poor households. Moreover, the burden of poverty falls disproportionately on a few groups -- African Americans, Hispanic Americans, Native Americans, Pacific Islanders and Asian Americans, women who head households, children, and persons with disabilities. African American and Hispanic American families are nearly three times more likely to be poor than white families, and the incidence of poverty is even higher among Native Americans. Growing numbers of homeless inhabit our streets. Because of poverty, millions of Americans are without adequate nutrition, health care and shelter.

On a global level, the overwhelming majority of the human family confront poverty, poor health, and lack of education. One in five live in absolute and dehumanizing poverty, facing a daily struggle to survive. Although the world food supply can provide enough for all, some 770 million people do not get sufficient food for an active and healthy life. Persistent hunger throughout the world dooms new generations of children to prolong problems caused by severe malnutrition at an early age. There are more adult illiterates, more unemployed, more persons suffering from ill health, and more people unable to satisfy their basic needs for food and clean water than there were 25 years ago.

The gap between degrading poverty and dazzling wealth has become evermore pronounced. In the U.S., the wealthiest 20 percent of all households own 75 percent of all assets and earn almost half of all income, and these shares have increased during the past decade. At a global level, the disparities in income are enormous and increasing. In 1983, 20 percent of the world's population received 68 percent of the world's income. Low income countries in Asia, Africa, and Central America, with nearly half the world's population, account for only five percent of global income. During the past ten years, standards of living in the poorest countries have fallen further behind.

B. RACISM

> The historical record of how white Europeans conquered North America by destroying the native population and how they then built their new nation's economy on the backs of kidnapped Africans who had been turned into chattel are facts that can hardly be denied...White America has yet to recognize the extent of its racism -- that we are and have always been a racist society -- much less to repent of its racial sins. (Jim Wallis, editor of Sojourners Magazine)

Racism is the systematized oppression of one race by another. In 1984, the National Council of Churches defined racism as "racial prejudice plus power." This position maintains that privileges conferred upon the majority by virtue of its racial origins, are supported by a self-sustaining system of institutions and structures which economically benefits from racism. Hence, the Commission for Racial Justice of the United Church of Christ defined racism as "economically-empowered racial prejudice and discrimination."

In specific terms, these policies translate into an unemployment rate in American Indian communities ranging from 70 to 90 percent. Alcoholism, and other forms of substance abuse, has touched about 90 percent of individuals in the American Indian community. Hispanic Americans, 85 percent of whom live in urban areas, are a disproportionately poor group living in substandard inner-city housing. The poverty rate for Hispanics was 28.2 percent in 1987, significantly higher than the already elevated rate of 21.9 percent in 1977. Over the last eight to ten years, poverty spread more rapidly among Hispanics than among any other group. Likewise, economic motivations played a role in the internment of Japanese-Americans during World War II, when war hysteria was used as a smokescreen for the stealing of land and other possessions. The majority of Japanese Americans in Hawaii were not put in concentration camps because most of them were lowly-paid pineapple and sugar plantation workers in 1942. Japanese Americans, however, owned land in California and were supplying approximately 90 percent of the vegetable crop in the state.

African Americans, who were forcibly brought to the U.S. as slaves, continue to suffer from economic exploitation. Their unemployment rate in 1986 was 14.5 percent as compared to a white unemployment rate of 6.0 percent. African Americans between ages 16-19 suffered a staggering rate of 39.3 percent. Today, whites enjoy 12 times the net worth of African-Americans. The median net worth of African-American households is $3,400, compared to $39,100 for white households. Unfortunately, Martin Luther King's words still apply till today: "There were slaves when [the Declaration of Independence] was written; there were slaves when it was adopted; and to this day, black Americans do have not life, liberty nor the privilege of pursuing happiness, and millions of poor white Americans are in economic bondage that is scarcely less oppressive."

C. MILITARIZATION

> In the councils of Government, we must guard against the acquisition of unwarranted influence, whether sought or unsought, by the military-industrial complex. The potential for the disastrous rise of misplaced power exists and will persist. (Dwight D. Eisenhower, January 17, 1961)

The fuel consumed by the Pentagon in a single year would run the entire U.S. public transit system for 22 years. For the cost of one stealth bomber ($516 million), we could construct 9,285 units of housing for low income families, the elderly and the handicapped. The world's annual military budget equals the income of 2.6 billion people in the 44 poorest nations. Military defense budgets in the Third World are about seven times as large as in 1960. More wars were fought in 1987 than in any previous year on record; four-fifths of the deaths in those wars were civilian.

Worldwide, nations devote an outrageous amount of their resources to the military sector, both to dominate other nations as well as to protect themselves. This massive diversion of the earth's limited resources, nearly one trillion dollars per year, involves nearly all nations, draining funds for internal development and basic human services. The competition between the United States and the Soviet Union has provided the major impetus for the arms race. The most rapid growth in military spending with the most pernicious consequences, however, has taken place in the Third World countries, where military outlays have increased seven-fold since 1960.

The U.S. government today is aligned with people and governments all over the world who want to keep power and wealth in the hands of the few. This policy is necessary to protect U.S. transnational global interests. Unfortunately for the majority of the people of the world, East-West conflicts have been effectively used by the U.S. military-industrial complex to obtain billions of dollars from U.S. taxpayers to maintain the injustices and privileges of the existing global economic order.

D. ECONOMIC DISLOCATION

> $3.35 an hour jobs don't come near to providing even the basics for three kids. I've working enough of them to know. (Selena Barr, mother of three from North Carolina)

In 1968, full time employment at minimum wage resulted in an income slightly above the poverty level for a family of three. In 1988, full time minimum wage employment yielded 74 percent of the poverty income level for a family of three.

In recent years, Americans have experienced the meaning of such terms as "economic dislocation," "capital flight," and "plant closures," as the character of the U.S. economy has been changed from a leading manufacturing to a corporate service economy. Since reaching a peak in 1973, real U.S. wages declined by 15 percent. The congressional Joint Economic Committee reports that 60 percent of all jobs created since 1979 pay less than $7,000 a year. Thus, government statistics are misleading, causing one to incorrectly assume that Americans have benefited by greater employment. Once the largest creditor nation, by 1986 the U.S. was the largest debtor nation. In the course of these major structural changes, declining farm prices and land values and the displacement of farmers by agribusiness in rural areas threaten to end widespread ownership of agricultural land by productive working farm families. Unregulated movement of jobs and capital between regions and across countries results in factory closings that leave individual workers without jobs and whole communities without a means of livelihood.

In the global economy many of these trends are accentuated. The internationalization of capital and the global scope of operations of transnational corporations give developing countries little control over major disruptions of their economies. Economic problems, whether recession, inflation, or changes in access to markets, produce a terrible toll in human suffering, particularly in the poorest and most vulnerable economies, and the burden of adjustment falls disproportionately on the poor. Since 1982, debtor countries have been paying more funds in debt servicing than they have received in new loans. In 1987, this negative capital flow exceeded 29 billion dollars.

E. ENVIRONMENTAL POLLUTION AND RESOURCE DEPLETION

> During the next three decades man will drive an average of 100 species to extinction everyday... The present rate is at least 1,000 times the pace that has prevailed since prehistory. Even the mass extinctions 65 million years ago that killed off the dinosaurs and countless other species did not significantly affect flowering plants... But these plant species are disappearing now, and people, not comets or volcanos, are the angels of destruction. Moreover, the earth is suffering the decline of entire ecosystems -- the nurseries of new life-forms... British ecologist Norman Myers has called it the "greatest single setback to life's abundance and diversity since the first flickerings of life almost 4 billion years ago." (Time Magazine, January 2, 1989)

A century of haphazardly producing and disposing of toxic wastes now endangers the earth's rivers, lakes, oceans, and air. Acid rain from the burning of fossil fuels imperils lakes, rivers, and forests, and comprises a health risk in some areas. Nuclear accidents and nuclear wastes threaten the life-supporting capacity of the earth. Increases in carbon dioxide levels from the burning of fossil fuels appear to be creating a global greenhouse effect that will significantly alter climatic conditions.

In 1987, the World Commission on Environment and Development commented that "humanity has the ability to make development sustainable -- to ensure that it meets the needs of the present without compromising the ability of future generations to meet their own needs. The concept of sustainable development does imply limits... but sustainable development requires meeting the basic needs of all and extending to all the opportunity to fulfil their aspiration for a better life. A world in which poverty is endemic will always be prone to ecological and other catastrophes."

F. POWERLESSNESS

> When I give food to the poor they call me a saint, when I ask why the poor have no food, they call me a communist. (Dom Helder Camara, when Archbishop of Recife, Brazil)

In the years since the inception of the global debt crisis, the standard of living has sharply deteriorated in most Third World countries. Do we dare ask why?

Standards of living in the poorest countries have fallen further behind during the last ten years as the global debt crisis has caused a devastating impact on debtor countries. Per capita consumption among the 17 most debt-troubled nations has fallen by 11 percent since 1980. A number of the poorest debtor countries have seen their real incomes plunge by as much as two-thirds during this period. Children are the first and most vulnerable victims. UNICEF estimates that 40,000 children die everyday from malnutrition and easily preventable diseases. Schools and health clinics are closing because of cuts in government social spending and the high cost of imported supplies.

At the global level the emergence of a global economy characterized by mutual interdependence and shared problems has not been accompanied by the creation of institutions and processes for dealing with these new economic realities. Poor countries are caught in a spiral of unstable and frequently declining prices for the agricultural commodities they export, with limited access to markets in industrialized countries, capital for investment, or new technology. The result is massive indebtedness of many Third World countries that further increases their vulnerability because even small changes in global interest rates or prices can change drastically their economic prospects. Moreover, the global debt crisis has eroded the sovereignty of indebted countries by giving the International Monetary Fund the power to demand major structural reforms and stringent austerity programs as the condition for extending financing to meet interest and debt payments.

Within the United States, many families and individuals feel they have little control over their own economic future. Distant economic policies and events result in high inflation or unemployment and threaten income security. Corporate decisions often have enormous impact on not only the workplace but entire communities. Indeed, we now live in an age where many middle class families find it increasingly difficult to balance the budget, and the poor live in an even more precarious situation in which any unforeseen economic problem may leave them homeless. In addition to homelessness, this has meant loss of health insurance coverage, family farm foreclosures, declining quality of life, an environment whose very ability to sustain life is threatened by human disasters and many other forms of what the Rev. Jesse Jackson termed "economic violence." Rising housing prices provide wealth to current homeowners, but exclude younger families from home ownership. A sense of economic helplessness creates stress and induces passivity, leading people to drop out of active participation in the social, political and economic organization of their communities.

V. THE MARKET ECONOMY: PROMISES AND PROBLEMS

As Christians we are called to participate in God's reign, by reshaping our human household in the light of our vision of a just economy. Through our covenant with God, we are responsible to God and to our sisters and brothers for the justice of the economic institutions in which we participate. That accountability is even greater in a democratic system through which each citizen retains the political voice to challenge harmful policies and to promote justice. In confronting and confessing the injustices that exist within our own economic institutions, we also express our conviction that God works with and through us to create a more just economic order.

Members of the United Church of Christ are part of a market-oriented economy, and citizens of an industrialized capitalist nation that shapes and often dominates the global market economy. We must name and challenge the economic injustices that exist within the United States' economic institutions and practices, not because we prefer an alternative form of economic organization, but because this is our household. It is where our responsibilities lie as North American Christians.

A market economy has certain strengths and certain weaknesses. Among the strengths of a market economy are:

1. Markets are especially useful given the limitations of human beings to foresee all the consequences of actions and complex policies. The price system is more sensitive to shifts in supply and demand than is centralized planning. Resource allocation and re-allocation is more flexible and nuanced, and often, more efficient.

2. Combined with a democratic political system, the market economy provides enormous freedom of choice for those who are able to participate in it fully. Those with the resources to purchase goods have a wide selection from which to decide. Those with access to education and training can choose their careers freely. When large numbers of persons participate as equals in the market, power and decision-making are dispersed. There is some empirical evidence that states with genuine political liberties are market oriented, although the reverse is not true.

3. Market economies are typically very productive. The profit incentives embedded in a market system encourage the production of a wide range of goods and services. Incentives always exist for producers to increase their productivity through new technologies, and more efficient use of workers and machines. Even a number of predominantly non-market economies, such as China, have recognized the advantage of allowing some competitive market forces to operate and provide vigor to the economic life of their nation.

4. A long history of economic growth and rising standards of living in market economies testify to the advantages of the market system for at least a portion of the population. In the U.S. since World War II, average hourly earnings adjusted for inflation have increased by 60 percent. However, it is also true that since 1970 average hourly earnings have been largely stagnant; increases in household income have occurred only because of an increase in the number of workers in the average household. In Japan and many of the market economies of Europe, capitalism combined with government policies have produced even higher rates of growth and higher and more widely distributed standards of living.

Juxtaposed against the vision of God's household, the suffering within our own household demonstrates that we face serious economic problems which markets have not alleviated. Not all of these problems are the direct result of the market system. Many of them result from the interactions of our market economy with a host of humanly constructed social and political institutions. Beyond this, Christian faith affirms that there are other factors than market factors which should motivate our economy, and other claims upon us, including the claims of conscience and of righteousness.

Standing beside the strengths of a market economy are these weaknesses:

1. The market system does not guarantee that the minimum resources needed to fulfill basic human needs will be available to all citizens. Market exchange cannot guarantee equity of social justice. In fact, when combined with already existing inequities of wealth or competence or other forms of social power, market exchange can become, for many, an exchange of desperation. Those who are excluded from or unable to participate in the labor market -- particularly children, elderly, handicapped, and persons with inadequate skills -- typically experience poverty, poor health, and inadequate housing. Even some who work full-time in the United States do not earn enough for adequate survival. Experience has demonstrated that economic growth alone is not enough to alleviate this problem. For instance, steady economic growth over the past five years has not reduced the poverty rate among minorities, and has not increased the earning power of many low-skilled workers.

2. Market exchange cannot count non-monetary costs and much of the vaunted efficiency of markets fails when a full cost-accounting does not occur. These uncounted costs, from pollution to the damage done to communities through capital movement, must be dealt with and compensated outside of the market.

3. Unchecked exchange leads not only to gross inequalities of income and wealth but also to concentration of economic power without adequate public accountability. These concentrations of power not only distort the price-system but also encroach on government, the courts, educational institutions and the family. For instance, the size and the economic resources of large transnational corporations provide them with some degree of independence from national government boundaries. Even within industrialized societies where national governments have regulated certain aspects of corporate behavior with varying degrees of success, regional administrations, local communities, and employees often have little influence on corporate behavior. Problems of public control and corporate accountability are magnified in poor countries, where the size and resources of transnational corporations often exceed that of the state.

4. A market economy emphasizes individual choice and often ignores the importance of public concerns. On the one hand, individual choices are shaped and bounded by the community environment in which they are made. For instance, within a corporate setting individuals often see only certain actions as acceptable or possible. An analysis that emphasizes individual choice but ignores the effects of the larger community upon that choice is fundamentally flawed. On the other hand, an emphasis solely on individual action ignores the importance of considering the welfare of the entire economic household. The Christian message clearly states that self-interest is not an adequate approach to all economic decisions. There are times when the needs of the larger community, whether that be a family, a church, or a nation, must take precedence over self-interest.

5. Market exchange is, by itself, indifferent to what is exchanged, and market systems will respond to military spending as well as the demand for Barbie dolls. A growing proportion of the budgets of both richer and poorer nations, a total of 15 trillion dollars since 1960, is going into military spending and away from human development. In a similar manner, the

international market for illegal drugs responds to a demand, but produces materials that destroy human beings. Deciding what should be produced and what should not requires social decision as well as individual decision. Moreover, protecting non-market spheres of life, such as family privacy, requires external restraint.

6. Market exchange encourages a society of mobility and consumption, often corrosive of community values. While it is true of other economies as well, market economies especially encourage false values and priorities. The accumulation of individual wealth and corporate profit is frequently the ultimate measure of success. This tempts people into believing that the accumulation of things is a primary measure of human worth and stature.

7. In the international arena, where markets often have even fewer restraints, the preceding effects are often exacerbated. The global market economy demonstrates even more clearly its inability to provide for the equitable distribution of resources. Although enough food can be produced worldwide for all humans to have a sufficient diet, serious problems of hunger and malnutrition exist around the world. The market does little to encourage the sharing and cooperation that would result in a better distribution of the world's resources. Many economic problems, such as pollution, labor migration, and international investment flows, are not limited by national boundaries. Economic policy decisions made by large nations such as the United States impact not only their own citizens, but have major effects on the lives of people around the globe who have little input into those decisions. Existing economic institutions cannot adequately respond to these cross-national economic forces.

These standard defects vary in their impact on different historical circumstances. In the U.S. they are exacerbated by historical patterns of racism and sexism and other forms of exclusion. Institutional prejudices, e.g., racism and sexism, limit the extent to which "free choice" actually operates for individuals of a different race, sex, religion, sexual orientation or nationality. Thus some people are consistently excluded from full participation in the economic household of our nation. Given the already alarming inequity of income and wealth, and the extraordinary numbers of marginal persons in our society, considerable restructuring must take place even for minimal justice. Moreover, the inequities and exclusion result in part from structural decisions already in effect, e.g., the "planned economy" of military expenditures, tax policies transferring income to corporations and other concentrations of economic power, the current incentives for corporate takeovers, and the penalizing of corporate savings and productive investment.

VI. STATEMENT OF CHRISTIAN CONVICTION

The UCC Statement of Mission reads: "Empowered by the Holy Spirit, we are called and commit ourselves... to praise God, confess our sin, and joyfully accept God's forgiveness..."

In that spirit, the members of the United Church of Christ, its instrumentalities, local churches, associations, conferences, and all national bodies confess that we live in a privileged society which has committed economic injustices in this nation and the world. We are called to confess that from places of privilege it is difficult to stand in solidarity with the poor and the oppressed.

We are called to confess that we have done too little to correct the economic injustices in the world.

We are called, in the Statement of Mission, to "name and confront the powers of evil within and among us." One of those powers is the worship of mammon (wealth) in all its forms, to which we have fallen prey.

Similarly, we are called to "repent our silence and complicity with the forces of chaos and death." Our silence and complicity contribute to the economic oppression of persons whom God loves.

Furthermore, we are called to live out the commandment of Jesus: "You shall love the Lord your God with all your heart, and with all your soul, and with all your mind, and with all your strength... you shall love your neighbor as yourself (Mark 12:29-31)" Love for our neighbor compels us to act.

As we confess and repent, we declare our intention to work and struggle for a nation and a world in which every human being is empowered to live life fully, joyfully, and in dignity.

A. MARKS OF A JUST ECONOMY

We affirm that to be involved in the transformation of economic life is an authentic Christian calling. Christ calls the Church to bear witness to God's sovereignty and presence among us. Christ calls us from the idolatries of greed and materialism to a full relationship with God, creation, and one another. Christ reveals God's suffering passion with the poor and uncovers God's reign of justice in our midst. In the practice of justice in the public economy the covenant of the human household with God is fulfilled and God is worshipped. Economic justice in God's household includes the following dimensions. They provide a standard by which to measure contemporary economic systems, as well as a vision which can guide and inspire efforts to create greater economic justice in today's world.

1. A just economy celebrates and serves the fundamental covenant purpose of human life, which is to love God and neighbor. The laws of economics are ultimately accountable to the law of God's love. The rules of the marketplace are not autonomous, but they are accountable to God's grace. Human beings do not live by bread alone. In view of the household God is seeking to create, the value of one's life is not measured by one's material possessions.

2. A just economy gives all persons access to the basic material necessities of life. When some people are excluded from the abundance of life which God intends for all persons, justice is denied. From its beginning the household of Jesus Christ has witnessed many evidences of injustice, including large numbers of people in need, and great gaps between rich and poor.

3. A just economy builds and enhances human communities of dignity and well-being. Only in actual human communities are mutual interdependence and dignity recognized. Economic policy should therefore serve to protect and strengthen such community. In a just economy, the division of labor reflects our mutual interdependence and underscores the importance of the participation of all human beings in the community. According to the new covenant in Christ, all individuals are committed to the well-being of the human household as part of their commitment to God.

4. A just economy is inclusive, involving all able people in responsible, participatory, and economically rewarding activity. Excluded from productive and

meaningful work and from the means of life, neither the individual nor the community can survive. Hence in a just economy, no one is unfairly disadvantaged or excluded from productive activity. Economic decision-making should reflect the needs and participation of all members of the community.

5. A just economy encourages creativity, skill, and diligence. Human productivity and a sense of vocation benefits all of society and provides a sense of accomplishment to individuals. The economic system should call forth the creative and creating nature of human beings.

6. A just economy assures equality of opportunity. Discrimination of any sort, whether based on such factors as race, class, age, ethnic origins, sexual orientation, physical disability, religion, or gender, contradicts the fundamental Christian affirmation of the equality and worth of all human beings. Discrimination denies the inclusiveness of the human community. When inequality and prejudice are embedded in societal and institutional processes, this constitutes a form of social sin. Justice requires a commitment to affirmative action and structural changes that redress the effects of discrimination, domination, and exploitation.

7. A just economy reflects God's passion for the poor and disadvantaged, enhancing the life opportunities of the poor, the weak, and groups at the margin of society. Indeed, in a truly just economy there will be no poor. Economic resources should be so distributed that all individuals are empowered to participate fully in the economic system. A just economy seeks continually to redress imbalances in wealth and power so that the poor and weak can take control of their lives and shape their own future.

8. A just economy recognizes the integrity, fullness, and sacredness of creation. Economic justice is understood to include environmental wholeness and an ethic that will ensure a sustainable future for the planet. Humanity is an integral part of an interrelated creation. To abuse, exploit, and deplete resources or cause species' extinction for economic gain violates the integrity of creation, and, therefore, is an act of destruction. With time, there will likely be few survivors of major sustained ecological abuse.

9. A just economy acknowledges the dignity of human beings as made known in Jesus Christ, and guarantees the basic human rights necessary to maintain the sacredness of individuals. Human dignity involves the recognition of each person as a decision-maker in the community, so that no one is deprived of an active voice. This means recognizing rights to political liberty and participation, and economic rights to food, shelter, and health care.

10. A just economy requires and promotes international peace and well-being. There is no genuine peace without justice, nor can there be justice without peace. In a just economy, the intent of production should center on improving the lives of all citizens, and not on the proliferation of weapons.

B. IMPLICATIONS

Confronted by the suffering and inadequacies of our current economy, we are impelled toward change, seeking to bring greater justice into our economic household. Many of us are deeply troubled by the economic inequities we see within our nation and the world, but also deeply fearful of what greater economic equity and justice might mean for our own lives. We are unwilling to depend upon God alone for our security, and are frightened that economic reform might mean less economic security for ourselves. Some who have been successful in the market economy may find it difficult to acknowledge that the very system that brought them rewards has treated others unjustly. Some whose economic situation is precarious may fear that change will only make things worse. Many would happily vote for reform if it meant that the poor would become middle-income, but are afraid that it might mean instead that the middle-income will become poor. All of these fears we must honestly bring before God. We must confess our lack of faith, and ask God's help in overcoming our fears. We must center our lives in God's abundant love. Through worship, praise, and prayer we can find the faith and courage that will enable us to fulfill our covenant with God, working toward an economy in which justice and peace prevail.

With a more faith-centered spirituality we prepare ourselves to actively seek both the cost and the joy of discipleship affirmed in the United Church of Christ Statement of Faith. As individuals this means evaluating our own lifestyles, to see if they are consistent with shared life in the household of God. We must find ways to educate and inform ourselves on the economic suffering of our neighbors and on possible ways in which we can help prevent such suffering in the future. An important part of this education involves talking with those whose economic perspectives differ from our own. We must actively seek out and openly listen to those who are the widow, the orphan, and the sojourner of our day. The Church is an important place in which this listening can occur, for it is the one place where people from all economic backgrounds gather together around the table in complete equality before God.

Changes in our own individual lives, however, while a crucial and necessary step, are not enough. Major institutional changes must also occur in the economy of our nation as well. While recognizing the strengths of the market, we must also realize its limits. We must develop mechanisms within the political system which supplement and reform some aspects of the market economy, rectifying economic injustices and increasing the ability of all individuals to be full economic participants. This requires joining together in citizen action. We recognize that there is no clear or easy way to move from biblical and theological mandates to particular policy recommendations. Yet we strongly affirm the following political and economic changes which address some of the injustices and problems in our current economy. We acknowledge that long-term efforts will be necessary to implement these approaches.

1. In order to create a country in which the promise of life, liberty, and the pursuit of happiness is fulfilled for each person, we are committed to achieving an economic "bill of rights" that will provide:

    -- A guaranteed national minimum income level, ensuring every person access to adequate food, clothing, and shelter;
    -- A non-discriminatory national health care program available to all persons;
    -- A quality education system that provides to every person nurture, enrichment, and education from infancy to adulthood;
    -- A right to employment consistent with each person's potential;
    -- A guaranteed right of every person to access housing that is permanent and affordable.

2. To further the promotion of human rights on a global level, we affirm the need for the implementation of the Universal Declaration of Human Rights, endorsed by the United

States 40 years ago, which calls all countries to recognize the economic, human and political rights of their citizens. To this end, we reiterate the appeal that the U.S. government ratify the Covenant on Economic, Social, and Cultural Rights and other human rights' conventions approved by the United Nations that are pending before the Senate.

3. To create a more democratic economic system in which all people participate and through which all are nurtured, we affirm the need for wider participation in ownership and management of economic institutions and for more inclusive and democratic patterns of decision-making in private and public organizations. Economic democracy may include greater use of democratic planning at local and national levels, as well as greater opportunities for worker participation in workplace decisions. Economic democracy also involves facilitating and empowering the poor, racial and ethnic peoples, women, low-income and disempowered groups to participate on a more equal basis in the political decision-making process. Further, economic democracy entails framing economic issues in ways that informed citizens can consider policy alternatives, make intentional decisions, and express their views.

4. We affirm the need to reorder national and global priorities away from military expenditures and toward a just peace economy, as stated in the Just Peace Pronouncement adopted by the Fifteenth General Synod. The ending of the Cold War now enhances the feasibility of moving from a national security to a just peace economy in which the promotion of human welfare and the elimination of poverty are our primary goals.

5. We affirm the need for public and private sector initiatives that encourage the development of community-based enterprises for creating jobs by meeting local needs such as housing and recreation, and which are accountable to local residents and organizations. Such community development corporations can be funded by government sources or by religious, labor, or other non-profit groups which may have endowment funds or pensions funds to invest.

6. We affirm the need for the development of mechanisms that increase the public accountability and responsibility of corporations and governmental agencies involved in economic decision-making.

7. We affirm the need to improve environmental stewardship by the United States and other countries to assure that economic development does not poison the rich abundance of creation for short-term monetary gain. Better stewardship entails intentional and consistent efforts to consider the long-term environmental implications in all economic planning and development and to take measures to protect our fragile ecosystem. Responsible stewardship also requires legally enforceable programs that regulate the use and disposal of toxic wastes and industrial hazards. We additionally support investment in the development and adoption of more sustainable technologies compatible with the needs of future generations. We support the need to strengthen cross-national organizations in their capacity to deal with global environmental issues.

8. We affirm the need for the entire global community to strengthen global economic institutions or establish new ones that will address cross-national economic concerns. In particular,

    a. World economic institutions, such as the International Monetary Fund or the International Bank for Reconstruction and Development, should be restructured to include greater participation on the part of poorer nations in their decisions, so that these institutions reflect the perspectives and needs of the poorer nations as well as the interests of richer countries;

b. New economic and financial institutions need to be developed to reach and empower the poor more directly;

c. More rational and equitable strategies should be designed to deal with debt problems at home and abroad. For developing countries this includes shifting the burden from the poor and sharing the responsibility for repayment more equitably among international banks, governments of the industrialized countries, and multilateral economic institutions. Such mechanisms could include ceilings on debt service based on ability to pay, refinancing arrangements to reduce repayment burdens, debt reduction, and major debt elimination in the poorest countries. The inability of poor nations to repay debt should not lead to exploitation by creditor nations;

d. Institutions should be developed that provide international regulation of the behavior of transnational private corporations and that support individual countries in their oversight of these organizations;

e. Equitable and secure ways of funding international institutions need to be actively pursued that will provide resources to address international problems and needs.

Certainly, judged against the vision of justice in the household of God, all current economic systems fall short and are unjust. These affirmations suggest a direction through which our existing economic systems can be transformed. We recognize that these affirmations, if implemented, would only be first steps toward full economic justice. Taken with God's help, they will move us closer to a household in which all may find abundance. As we progress in this struggle, however, we will necessarily recognize new and additional tasks that need to be undertaken and that demand our attention and support. The Church should be actively involved in envisioning ways in which greater economic justice can be achieved.

Called by Christ to participate in God's reign, the Church must take a leadership role in the movement toward greater economic justice for the whole human household. Thus, the Church must become a model of economic justice in its own institutional practices. This will require reviewing and reforming its internal economy to reflect an active concern with issues of economic equity and justice, supporting the struggles of the poor throughout the world, and encouraging the formation of Christian communities which practice resource sharing and income equity and which encourage advocacy and action with the poor.

The Church should also invite Christians to review and reform their own individual lives, taking God's grace and God's reign as the central source and purpose of life.

Finally, the Church must continue to affirm the vision of justice and peace to which all faithful Christians are called. It must actively preach God's reign of suffering love within the human household. Within the Church, individuals and groups from different economic backgrounds can worship together as equals with a common confession to one faith. The Church provides a place where reconciliation and recognition of common interests can begin to emerge. The Proposal for Action which accompanies this Pronouncement provides a plan whereby the United Church of Christ can begin to implement this vision.

A PROPOSAL FOR ACTION ON CHRISTIAN FAITH: ECONOMIC LIFE AND JUSTICE

"A Proposal for Action is a recommendation of specific directional statements and goals implementing a Pronouncement."

I. SUMMARY

This Proposal for Action affirms the United Church of Christ's commitment to be actively concerned with justice in our economic institutions and daily economic lives. It delineates the strategies and specific actions by which all parts of the United Church of Christ (individuals, local churches, instrumentalities, conferences, associations and seminaries) can work for economic justice as an imperative of our affirmation and understanding of the Christian faith.

II. BACKGROUND STATEMENT

This Proposal for Action is based upon the proposed Pronouncement on Christian Faith: Economic Life and Justice. The proposed Pronouncement on Christian Faith: Economic Life and Justice is a synthesis of two proposed Pronouncements submitted to the Seventeenth General Synod. This Proposal has been developed in response to the request of the Fourteenth General Synod to engage in a study of economics and theology, and to recommend an appropriate response by the United Church of Christ.

The proposed Pronouncement on Christian Faith and Economic Life has been informed by feedback to the study paper, Christian Faith and Economic Life, provided by a diverse group of United Church of Christ members. The racial and ethnic members of the United Church of Christ felt that the issue of racism in the context of envisioning appropriate economic life from a Christian faith perspective needed further articulation; this was provided in the proposed Pronouncement on Christian Faith and Economic Justice. The Seventeenth General Synod celebrates the active involvement of diverse groups in the discussion and formulation of proposed statements on the highly complex issues of Christian faith and economics presented in these two documents. Hence, the Seventeenth General Synod celebrates the fulfillment of the United Church of Christ's motto: "that they may all be one."

The synthesized Pronouncement presents policy statements for the United Church of Christ on the issue of economic justice. This Proposal for Action, therefore, delineates a specific program of action strategies that will enable the United Church of Christ to become effectively involved at all levels in the struggle to ensure that economic justice is a reality for all of God's people in the United States and throughout the world.

This Proposal for Action further seeks to implement, through Christian social action, the programmatic thrust of the Pronouncement on Christian Faith: Economic Life and Justice which seeks to remain faithful to the Statement of Faith and the Statement of Mission of the United Church of Christ.

III. DIRECTIONAL STATEMENTS AND GOALS

"God calls the worlds into being, creates persons in God's image, and sets before each one the ways of life and death... "

Our lives are derived from and lived in relationship with God. Our joy is to live in covenant with God and one another in God's household. Our delight is to use freely and faithfully the gifts of God who is Creator.

"In Jesus Christ, the man of Nazareth, our crucified and risen Savior, God has come to us... "

As people of the United Church of Christ, affirming our Statements of Faith and Mission, we seek within the Church Universal to participate in God's mission of economic justice for all of God's peoples and to follow the liberating way of the crucified and risen Christ ...

We have confessed and stated our Christian conviction to struggle against all forms of economic injustice in this nation and throughout the world ...

We establish as a goal the just transformation of the market economy into an economic system that fundamentally ensures economic, environmental, gender, racial and social justice and equality in the United States ...

We further establish as a goal the just transformation of the global economy into an economic order that fundamentally ensures economic, racial and social justice for all of God's peoples throughout the world ...

To acknowledge God's reign is to shape on earth a community capable of the humanity exemplified in Jesus Christ and to take the suffering love of God made known in the life, crucifixion, and resurrection of Jesus as the model for a covenant household of justice and love. Thus, God's reign does not mean to flee the rigors of earth and seek some heavenly holiness, rather is sought through service, advocacy, and covenant.

Based on this confession and affirmation, the Seventeenth General Synod calls for the adoption of the following actions.

IV. CALL TO MEMBERS

The Seventeenth General Synod calls members to develop a faith-oriented understanding of economic life by engaging in:

1. Regular public worship, the center and foundation of Christian life, which renews our covenant with God to seek justice in God's household;
2. Prayer and spiritual discipline, to strengthen the struggle for economic justice, which includes tithing or giving to share resources with those who have less;
3. Theological reflection on the basic tenets of Christian Faith to understand better the imperatives of God's mission of economic justice;
4. Efforts to adopt a personal and family lifestyle consistent with life in the household of God and God's creatures;

5. Personal contact with and listening to individuals of other races, classes, income levels, economic backgrounds, and nationalities;

6. Personal initiatives and voluntary service to promote economic justice, including involvement in the political process.

V. CALL TO LOCAL CHURCHES

The Seventeenth General Synod calls local churches and their members to respond to the call for economic justice in their worship and education activities, financial decisions, and social outreach.

1. Worship and Spiritual Concerns: We call churches to:

   a. preach on God, giver of abundant creation, who is a lover of justice and creation, and on the justice-seeking ministry of Christ. This includes regularly incorporating visions of economic justice into public worship;

   b. encourage all members to pray, meditate, and engage in those spiritual disciplines that help relate Christian faith to economic life;

   c. minister to and support those members struggling to live just Christian lives in their work environments, as well as those members and families who are struggling to transform their personal lifestyles and commitments to be more consistent with seeking justice and wholeness in God's household.

   d. implement a program of Christian education that informs and challenges us to knowledge of economic injustices and to commitments to develop more just economic structures and systems.

2. Study and Education: We call churches to engage in study and educational programming that will enable their members better to reflect on and act for economic justice. We call churches to:

   a. establish study groups to engage in Bible study, and to utilize the foregoing Pronouncement, the study paper Christian Faith and Economic Life, and other documents that relate Christian faith to economic life and the economy of the environment;

   b. study the economy of their local communities, analyze local economic inequities and injustices, identify the social forces, conditions and the policies which contribute to economic suffering, and explore ways their church can address these problems. This may include providing opportunities for dialogue between people of different economic backgrounds;

   c. seek out churches of different racial and economic backgrounds and engage in study and dialogue with them on issues of economic justice;

   d. increase members' awareness of global economic issues and the concerns and perspectives of persons around the world on these issues. This may include explicitly studying the differing views of the advantages and disadvantages of the market economy held by people who have suffered or benefited from the promises and problems of the market;

e. support and encourage church members regarding their own economic pain and problems.

3. An Economic Audit of the Church: We call local churches to examine critically the economy of their own church. We call churches to:

a. invest church endowment funds and other church investments in a manner consistent with the economic justice commitments of the United Church of Christ. This means careful attention to the policies of the financial managers, the financial institutions, and the issuers of securities that are selected, as well as active monitoring of the investment decisions made by church managers and/or church oversight committees;

b. examine the extent to which the church budget provides equitably for the salaries, pensions, and benefits of all church staff;

c. examine and make sure that the church budget reflects a serious commitment to promote economic justice in the community and the world;

d. study and adopt procedures in the institutional lifestyle of the church that are consistent with life in the household of God, including regular self-examination of the extent to which the church is focusing on acquisitive and materialistic patterns of behavior, often reflected in an overemphasis on such items as cushions, carpets, or organs;

e. implement just church policies for hiring and firing of staff, with particular attention to the hiring of minorities and women;

f. examine purchasing practices with attention to the equal employment and affirmative action practices of suppliers and vendors;

g. audit church property and equipment for responsible energy use, resource conservation, recycling practices, sound land use, and less polluting forms of transportation.

4. Advocacy for Economic Justice: We call local churches to:

a. join and participate actively in the Justice and Peace Network of the United Church of Christ, and the Network for Environmental and Economic Responsibility, and in interfaith advocacy organizations such as IMPACT and Interfaith Action for Economic Justice;

b. work on economic injustices within the local community and support community organizations that enhance the life opportunities and political voice of poor and minority groups, and that increase local economic control;

c. interpret, support, and participate in the work for economic justice conducted by the Conferences, and the national boards and instrumentalities of the United Church of Christ.

VI. CALL TO UNITED CHURCH OF CHRIST INSTRUMENTALITIES, CONFERENCES, ASSOCIATIONS AND SEMINARIES

The Seventeenth General Synod calls national United Church of Christ instrumentalities, Conferences, Associations, and the closely related seminaries of the United Church of Christ to respond to the call for economic justice through education, institutional change, and advocacy.

1. The Economy of the United Church of Christ. We call the United Church of Christ to work for economic justice by transforming its own internal organizational structure to conform to life in the household of God, so it reflects a commitment to economic justice. We call the United Church of Christ to:

   a. establish or commission existing committees for economic justice at the Association and Conference levels;

   b. sponsor research and development of a critical analysis of current economic justice issues and make recommendations for economic structures and systems that ensure economic justice for all people;

   c. examine and, where appropriate, encourage change in the distribution of income and resources among Conferences and Associations as well as between wealthier and poorer churches, seeking greater sharing based on mission and need;

   d. continue to promote socially responsible investment of the endowments and pensions of congregations, Conferences and instrumentalities. Where appropriate to the charter of the investment funds, the United Church of Christ should encourage greater use of investments that address economic justice objectives, but may entail greater risk or lower yields;

   e. examine equity in salaries, pensions, and benefits paid to United Church of Christ employees, and design structures that address current inequities;

   f. establish national and regional programs and projects that seek economic justice in the United States and in the world;

   g. assure that policies for hiring and firing of staff are just with particular attention to the hiring of minorities and women;

   h. confront racism and sexism within the church, strengthening the affirmative action activities of the denomination;

   i. reorient the interpretation, promotion, funding patterns, and priorities of mission programs to reflect the United Church of Christ's commitment to economic justice;

   j. develop ways to involve more people from the local church level, particularly from poor and minority communities, in the decision-making and budgeting process of the denomination.

2. Study and Education:

   a. We call upon all Instrumentalities and other National bodies to research and publish critical and constructive analysis of present economic structures and systems and make recommendations for just economic structures and systems;

   b. We call closely related seminaries of the United Church of Christ to participate in the development of a theology which demonstrates the relevance of biblical faith to economic systems and practices in the world and which affirms the wholeness of God's creation. Seminaries should be encouraged to offer courses that give students in the ministry a grounding in economics and economic justice, as well as provide similar continuing education opportunities for clergy and concerned lay people;

   c. We call the appropriate United Church of Christ instrumentalities to collect or develop and distribute curriculum materials which foster the study of economic justice issues by youth and adults in local churches;

   d. We call the national bodies of the United Church of Christ, along with Conferences and Associations, to develop seminars, and other programs that provide for the study of economic justice issues;

   e. We call the Office for Church in Society, the United Church Board for World Ministries, the United Church Board for Homeland Ministries, the Commission for Racial Justice and the Council for Racial and Ethnic Ministries to encourage the study of the Pronouncement on Christian Faith: Economic Life and Justice and of supporting documents. These groups are encouraged to appoint a task force to expand this pronouncement into a fuller study resource, similar to A Just Peace Church, and, in cooperation with Conferences and Associations, to conduct a church-wide study process;

   f. We call the Stewardship Council to develop a Sunday bulletin back page series which tells stories of economic justice and injustice, and relates these issues to biblical faith, and to utilize other means of communicating economic justice themes such as mission moments and offering material.

   g. We call all bodies of the Church to provide for study opportunities and dialogue which mix people across economic, racial, and national lines, providing the opportunity for all groups in the Church to listen to the concerns of those whose perspectives differ.

3. Advocacy for Economic Justice: We call the various bodies of the United Church of Christ, under the leadership of the Office for Church in Society, to increase their advocacy efforts on behalf of economic justice in the economic life of this nation and the international community. We call OCIS, BWM, BHM and CRJ to:

   a. lobby for legislative efforts that embody the policy proposals in Section VI of the foregoing Pronouncement;

   b. continue efforts to develop the Justice and Peace Network, placing emphasis on issues of economic justice and their links with peace issues;

   c. initiate efforts to develop an eco-justice advocacy network to address the linkage between economic and environmental justice issues;

d. empower churches and individuals to effectively organize and to change conditions of poverty;

e. gather poor people in conferences and hearings, so that their stories may be heard within churches, and the media, and Congress;

f. continue to advocate divestment from all corporations doing business in South Africa and other nations where economic and racial oppression are commonplace;

g. continue to advocate for the medically indigent and physically disabled due to catastrophic illnesses such as AIDS.

4. Ecumenical Initiatives: We call the Office of the President to take the initiative in approaching the National Conference of Catholic Bishops and the major Protestant denominations that have written public theologies of economics to discuss the development of an ecumenical statement on economic justice that would address the nation.

VII. CALL TO PARTICIPATION IN THE GLOBAL COMMUNITY

The Seventeenth General Synod calls upon all members, congregations, Associations, Conferences, instrumentalities, and related institutions in the United Church of Christ to recognize that we are members of a global community in which a majority of our brothers and sisters are poor. There is a need within this global community to create a new household, bearing one another's burdens and sharing God's gift of life together. To stand with God in solidarity with all people, particularly the poor and oppressed, and to challenge the value systems of this world, we call all parts of the United Church of Christ to:

1. Recognize the existence of one interdependent and global household and one mutually responsible people. This includes support of grassroots people's movements involved in the struggle for justice, peace, and full human development;

2. Participate in extensive people-to-people and congregational exchanges through the United Church Board for World Ministries, providing direct exposure to the situations and problems of churches and individuals in poorer countries;

3. Provide greater support to the ministries of partner churches, social service and relief programs, Christian seminaries, and educational, environmental and health institutions in poorer countries;

4. Participate in and support the World Council of Churches and other international interfaith institutions;

5. Invest in alternative financial institutions, such as the Ecumenical Development Cooperative Society, or other lending arrangements which promote socially desirable goals, such as housing, community economic development, or projects initiated by the poor;

6. Solicit the participation of partner churches into United Church of Christ structures and mission programs;

7. Develop new and more effective programmatic relationships with sisters and brothers in the Third World that enhance the global struggle toward economic justice;

8. Provide national and international leadership toward the development of an effective global ecumenical movement for economic justice which has as its central goal the just transformation of the global economic order.

VIII. IMPLEMENTATION

The Seventeenth General Synod requests that the Office for Church in Society, in consultation with the United Church Board for World Ministries, the United Church Board for Homeland Ministries, the Commission for Racial Justice and the Council for Racial and Ethnic Ministries, coordinate the implementation of this Proposal for Action through a broadly representative inter-agency and church-wide committee and make a detailed report to the Eighteenth and succeeding General Synods.